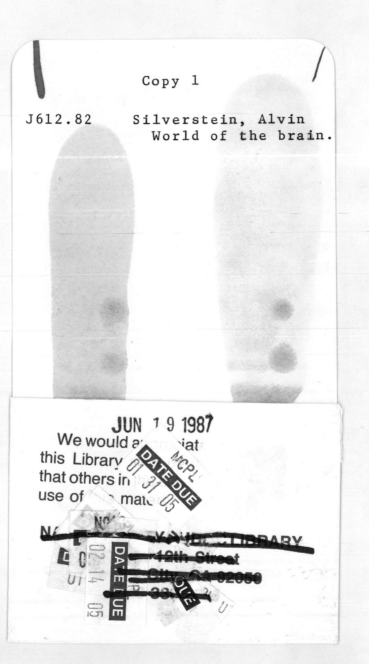

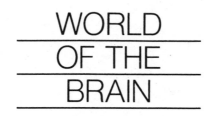

WORLD
OF THE
BRAIN

WORLD

OF THE

BRAIN

ALVIN AND VIRGINIA SILVERSTEIN

ILLUSTRATED BY WARREN BUDD

WILLIAM MORROW AND CO., INC.
NEW YORK

PHOTO CREDITS: Permission for the following photographs is gratefully acknowledged: Brookhaven National Laboratory and New York University, p. 49; Hunterdon Medical Center, Flemington, NJ, pp. 39 (Robert Alan), 41 both; Maimonides Hospital, Brooklyn, NY, pp. 52, 55 (both Dr. Stanley Krippner); National Institutes of Health Clinical Center, Department of Nuclear Medicine, p. 47; Technicare Corporation, pp. 43, 45; U.S. Public Health Service, p. 143.

Printed in the United States of America.

1   2   3   4   5   6   7   8   9   10

Library of Congress Cataloging-in-Publication Data

Silverstein, Alvin.
World of the brain.

Summary: Describes the physical structure, and
functions of the brain and the nervous system.
Also discusses various mental disorders, their
causes, and their treatment.
1. Brain—Juvenile literature.   2. Neurophysiology—
Juvenile literature.   [1. Brain.   2. Nervous system]
I. Silverstein, Virginia B.   II. Title.
QP376.S593   1986   612'.82   85-31007
ISBN 0-688-05777-2

For Linda Babeu

CONTENTS

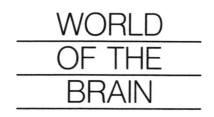

WORLD
OF THE
BRAIN

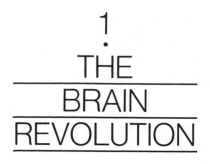

1
THE
BRAIN
REVOLUTION

When you look at yourself in the mirror, you see a familiar face. Those eyes, that nose and mouth, the shape of the jawline—you have seen them so many times. Just a glimpse, and you immediately recognize the face and think to yourself, "That's me."

Yet are you really just a face? What if you went to a plastic surgeon, who changed the shape of your nose, the tilt of your eyes, the line of your jaw? A different face would stare out of the mirror at you, but you would still feel like the same person inside.

What makes a person unique? It is the brain. It doesn't look like much. The size of a large grapefruit, this organ weighs about three pounds. The soft, jellylike substance of the brain is a pale tan color, covered with a pattern of ridges and grooves. It is hard to believe that this simple-looking mass of tissue holds the key to thoughts, memories, emotions, creativity—the very things that make us human. Spaceships, computers, paintings, music—every aspect of our civilization is a creation of human brains.

The study of how the brain works has become one of the most exciting frontiers of biomedical research. The rewards of a complete understanding of the brain would stagger the imagination. If we could learn how to utilize more of the brain's capacity, or even to expand that capacity, the discoveries that would follow would transform our world into a healthier, more comfortable, and more stimulating place.

Recent years have brought a revolution in ways of looking at the brain that have yielded a flood of new information about this amazing organ. New scanning machines such as the *CAT* and *MRI scanners* can give us a picture of a "slice" of the brain in fine detail that would be invisible on an ordinary X ray. Without surgery, one of these machines can pinpoint the site of damage after a head injury or a small cancerous tumor growing deep inside the brain. Another kind of scanner, the *PET scanner*, provides pictures of the brain in action. When a person sings a song or eats an orange or remembers a scene from childhood, different areas of the brain light up on the PET scan in a vivid color display. PET scanners also can reveal telltale patterns of brain activity that help doctors diagnose different forms of mental illness or determine whether an elderly person's forgetfulness is just a normal part of aging or a symptom of the dreaded Alzheimer's disease. Sophisticated new techniques of analysis have revealed a whole family of brain chemicals whose existence was not even suspected a decade or two ago. The use of computers with electrodes allows researchers to make detailed recordings of the brain's own electrical activity, and microelectrodes and fine-tuned chemical probes make it possible to study the effects of stimulating a single nerve cell. All these revolutionary new tools and techniques are helping researchers follow the flows of chemicals and electricity that determine thought, fear, memory, decision, creativity, and all the aspects of human personality.

With this new knowledge come some awesome possibilities for intervening not only to cure disease, but also perhaps to control and change the very essence of our humanity. These new abilities will bring a need for some equally awesome moral decisions. In the pages that follow, we shall explore the current state of our knowledge of the brain, the body's most crucial and mysterious organ, and the implications of the ongoing revolution in brain research for the future.

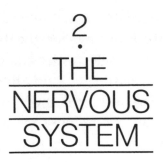

2
THE
NERVOUS
SYSTEM

Catching a ball, eating an orange, reading a book—all these are everyday activities that we can do without particularly thinking about them. Yet each of these seemingly simple actions actually involves a complex sequence of observations, decisions, and movements requiring a symphony of coordinated activity inside the body. The conductor of the symphony is the brain, which receives a continual flow of information from strategic outposts (the eyes, ears, and other sense organs), evaluates the data, makes decisions, and sends a new flow of messages outward to activate muscles or glands—all within a split second. The brain, and the network of nerves that act as communication lines to connect it with the body's organs for observing and acting, together make up the nervous system. This is the system that controls and coordinates all the body's activities.

Take catching a baseball, for example. As the leather-covered sphere hurtles toward you, your eyes follow its

THE NERVOUS SYSTEM

path. Messages race along nerves connecting your eyes to your brain, and the information on what you see is evaluated to inform you on the ball's speed, path, and how quickly it should reach you. Meanwhile, messages are speeding out along other nerves to signal muscles to move your head and eyeballs to keep the ball in sight, lift your hands up into position to snatch the ball in its flight, close your fingers around it to hold it securely, and brace the rest of your body so that the force of the ball's sudden stop won't knock you off balance.

Eating an orange has its own complexities. Dozens of pairs of muscles are signaled to contract and relax in sequence as your fingers deftly pluck off pieces of orange peel, split the juicy fruit in half, pull off a segment, and lift it toward your mouth. Meanwhile, your eyes have been transmitting pictures of the orange to your brain, and sensory cells in the lining of your nose have been sending their own messages about the fruit's distinctive smell. Even before the first orange segment is in your mouth, the brain has alerted the salivary glands in your mouth, and they have started pouring forth their watery secretions, which will help to mold the food into easily swallowed masses and start off the digestive processes. Muscles in your jaw contract and relax as you chew, your tongue moves nimbly to keep pushing the orange pulp into position for crunching teeth, and, with a final shove from your tongue and a convulsive contraction of throat muscles, the chewed-up orange goes sliding down toward your stomach. These movements, too, are controlled and coordinated by the brain.

Even reading a book is a far from simple action. Tiny movements of your eyeballs send your gaze jumping along one line and down to the next. The shapes of letters and words are perceived and analyzed, their individual meanings are compared with memories of past encounters, and they are put together into increasingly complex ideas. These, in turn, may recall experiences or give rise to new ideas. To an observer you might seem quiet, almost motionless, and yet there is a turmoil of activity going on in your brain.

THE NERVOUS SYSTEM

The body's nervous system has been compared to a vast telephone network that provides communications links with all parts of a big city. The brain can be viewed as a central switchboard, routing all the incoming and outgoing calls. But it is far more than this, for it also makes decisions about what is best for the body at any particular moment and what actions need to be taken to achieve it. The brain is thus also like the mayor of the city and its whole administrative staff.

Messages are carried along a telephone wire by electricity, and electricity flows at the speed of light, or about 186,000 miles per second. Electricity also is involved in the transmission of messages along the nerves of the body, but they travel far more slowly, generally from one to perhaps a couple of hundred miles per hour. That seems quite slow compared to the speed of electricity, but it is good enough for the body's needs. A message can travel along the nerves of your body, from the top of your head to the tip of your toe, in just about one-fiftieth of a second.

Nerve transmissions can take longer, though, when the messages must be thought over and decided inside the brain; but this time lag for processing might be too long in a real emergency. If you touch a hot iron, you jerk your hand away almost instantly, without consciously thinking of what you are doing. Only afterward do you become aware of what has happened. Then you may let out a loud "Ouch!" and perhaps put your finger into your mouth. Automatic actions, like pulling your hand away from a hot surface, are called *reflex actions.* They bypass the brain and are handled directly by the *spinal cord,* a shiny rope of nerves that runs down the length of the body. As soon as nerves from your finger carry the message "Hot!" to your spinal cord, this coordinating center sends its own messages along another set of nerves to the muscles in your arm to cause you to move it. At the same time, messages are relayed to the brain to inform it about the threatening situation; but, by the time these messages are sorted out, your arm is already moving, and you are out of danger. If you had to wait for your brain to direct *all* actions, you might get a bad burn. (Messages from the brain are responsible for the "Ouch!" reaction and prompt you to examine your hand for damage and to consider first-aid measures.)

The brain and the spinal cord (the control and coordination centers of the body) together form the *central nervous system.* Without them, the body could not function. The spinal cord transmits messages to and from the brain, in addition to handling some actions on its own. Damage to the spinal cord can cause paralysis, preventing the arms or legs or other body parts from moving. If the brain is destroyed, death comes instantly. And even if only certain parts of the brain are damaged, any kind of meaningful life may stop: the person just lies there, without seeing or hearing or thinking, although the heart goes on beating and the lungs continue breathing.

The brain and spinal cord are normally well protected from injury. Down its entire length, the spinal cord is en-

THE NERVOUS SYSTEM

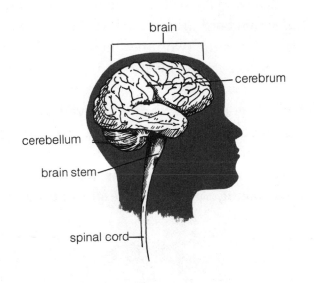

brain

cerebrum

cerebellum

brain stem

spinal cord

The human central nervous system consists of the brain and spinal cord.

closed in a flexible bony tube, the *spinal column*. This is made up of a series of bony rings jointed together so that you can bend and turn easily. At the top of the spinal column, the brain has its own bony case to protect it. This is a rigid, bowllike covering called the skull, or *cranium*. Inside their bony protections, both the brain and the spinal cord are wrapped in a set of three membranes, one inside the other, called the *meninges*. The outermost membrane, the *dura mater*, is a tough protective casing. (Dura means hard.) The middle membrane, the *arachnoid* membrane, is thin and delicate, like a spiderweb. (Arachnoid comes from a word meaning spider.) The innermost membrane, the *pia mater*, forms a soft and delicate covering for the brain and spinal cord. (Pia means tender.) A liquid filling the space between the two inner meninges helps to cushion the soft structures inside and protect them from shocks and blows.

Inside the bony cranium and the covering membranes, the human brain looks very much like the meat of a walnut (if you could imagine a walnut the size of a grapefruit). Viewed from above, it has just about the same shape as a walnut, with the same division into two dis-

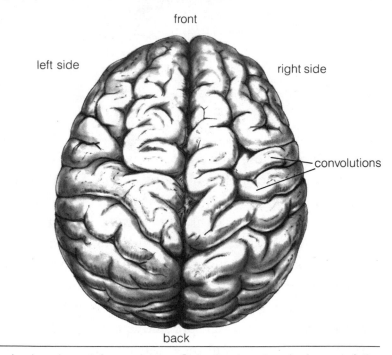

The brain, viewed from above. Only the two hemispheres of the cerebrum can be seen.

tinct halves and a surface that is scored and puckered into an intricate pattern of grooves and ridges. Unlike the walnut meat, however, it is not hard but rather soft and jellylike. This part of the brain is called the *cerebrum*. It is very important, being the part most responsible for the thoughts, memories, and personality traits that make us human. Nestled under the back of the cerebrum is another brain structure, also in two halves and also with a surface patterned by grooves and ridges. This is the *cerebellum*, which plays an important role in coordinating body movements. (Cerebrum comes from a Latin word meaning brain; the cerebellum is the "little brain.") Buried deep within the brain are a number of other structures that play interesting and important roles in the body's activities. The interior of the brain also contains some fluid-filled spaces called *ventricles*, which provide additional cushioning for the soft tissues. The base of the brain merges smoothly with the top of the spinal cord, with no clear dividing line to say where one ends and the other begins.

The brain and spinal cord are linked with the rest of the body by the network of nerves called the *peripheral nervous system*. Some nerves carry messages to the brain and spinal cord from the eyes, ears, nose, tongue, and other sense receptors. These nerves are called *sensory nerves*. Without them you could not see a bird flying, hear a train whistle, smell or taste a sizzling steak, or feel the roundness of an apple with your fingers. Other nerves carry messages from the brain and spinal cord to the

WORLD OF THE BRAIN

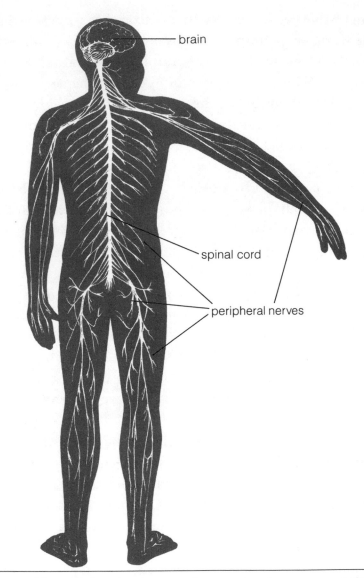

— brain

spinal cord

peripheral nerves

Nerves of the peripheral nervous system reach out to every part of the body.

THE NERVOUS SYSTEM

muscles of the body, the glands, and various other structures. Because many of these messages are instructions for movements, the nerves that carry messages away from the central nervous system are called *motor nerves.* They help you to walk and run, throw a ball, write a letter, and chew your food. Each nerve carries messages in only one direction—either to or from the brain—never both ways.

The nerves of the body are bundles of tiny threadlike nerve cells called *neurons.* Each one looks something like a thread with a knot in it, with its end starting to unravel. The "knot" is the *cell body,* which contains the nucleus that directs the nerve cell's activities. The "unraveled threads" that extend from the cell body are called *dendrites.* They look like the branches of a tree. (Dendrite comes from a word meaning tree.) The single long, slim branch that grows out from the cell body is called the *axon.* This is the part of the neuron that looks most like a thread. There is usually one axon in a nerve cell, and it ends in a cluster of branches called *terminal branches.* Messages are picked up by the dendrites and then transmitted to other cells along the axon. Some of the neurons of the legs may be as much as three feet long, but they are so thin that they cannot be seen without a microscope.

In addition to the neurons, the brain also contains a type of cell called the *glia.* Glial cells (from a Greek word meaning glue) hold the nerve cells together, support them, and help to insulate them. They also feed them since, unlike other cells of the body, neurons cannot take

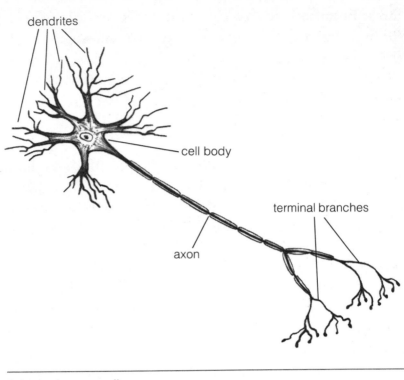

A typical nerve cell.

their nourishment directly from the blood vessels. Glial cells outnumber the neurons in a ratio of about ten to one.

Both sensory and motor nerve cells generally are wrapped together in bundles. Together they are known as the *peripheral nerves*. In the brain neurons are jumbled together in complex, interconnecting networks. Estimates of the number of neurons in the brain range from about ten billion to one hundred billion. That seems like an astonishing degree of uncertainty, but it is not surprising. No one could possibly hope to count all the neurons in a brain, and estimates are based on small samples of brain tissue.

If you have ever played with an electric train set, you probably discovered that you could join the branching sections of track together in a variety of ways to send the train along a number of different pathways. Imagine the number of different pathways that could be formed by the hookups of billions of neurons in the brain, each of which might have more than a thousand tiny branches! (The number of possible combinations adds up to more than the total number of atoms in the universe.) It is this fantastic possibility for different associations and pathways that permits the brain to process all the information from the senses; to store away memories of words and faces, a telephone number, the smell of a baking cake; to bring these facts back to mind almost instantly; and to combine them into new ideas that no one in the world has ever had before.

The messages that flash along the nervous system are carried by tiny individual neurons. At first it was thought that these messages were carried by currents of electricity like those that flow along telephone wires. Indeed, if electrical pickups are placed over the skull and on various other parts of the body, tiny pulses of electric current can be detected. However, as scientists worked out techniques and instruments for studying individual nerves and even individual neurons, they discovered that the body's message system is far more complicated.

Electricity is involved in the work of the neurons, but chemical reactions also play an important role. Chemical reactions in one part of the nerve fiber produce electric charges, and these charges in turn start off a chemical reaction in the next part of the fiber. In this way, the *nerve impulse* is carried along the nerve fiber.

A message in a neuron starts at the end of one of the branching dendrites and travels along past the cell body and down the axon. Nerve cells always transmit messages in that direction only: from dendrite to axon, never the reverse. The wave of electrochemical reactions passes down the axon into its terminal branches, which are in contact with the dendrites (or sometimes the cell bodies) of other neurons. These points of contact are called *synapses*. There is something surprising about the synapses: there is no actual physical connection between two neurons in a chain or network. Instead, there is a tiny fluid-filled gap between them. So the wave of electrochemical reactions cannot flow straight from one neuron into the next. It stops at the end of the terminal branch, where it triggers a new kind of reaction. Tiny sacs filled with chemicals called *neurotransmitters* are stimulated to burst open. The chemicals they contain spill out and move through the fluid across the synapse. When they reach the dendrite of the next neuron, they spark a new electrochemical reaction. The result of this reaction depends on two things: the kind of neurotransmitter involved and the nature of the spot on the receiving neuron (a structure

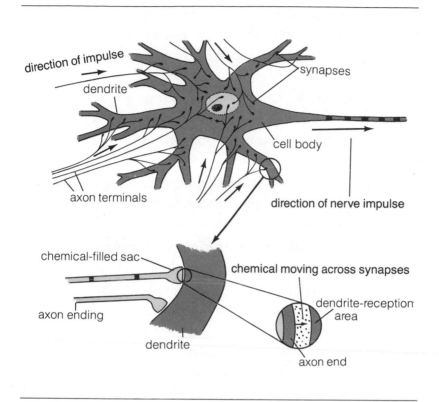

The nerve impulse is transmitted along the nerve cell from dendrite to axon and then carried across the synapse by chemical neurotransmitters.

called a *receptor*) that picks up the neurotransmitter. Usually the chemical messenger stimulates the next neuron in the chain to "fire" in turn, sending the message along in a new wave of electrochemical reactions. In such cases the neurotransmitter has a *stimulatory* effect. But sometimes there is an *inhibitory* effect: The neurotransmitter chemicals travel across the synapse and are picked up by receptors, and the neurons that received them become unable to react. They may not fire even if they are receiving stimulatory messages from the axons of other neurons.

Inhibition might seem to be working against itself, but it is very important in protecting the brain and helping it work effectively. Without inhibition, the brain would be swamped by such a constant flood of information that it would not be able to sort out what is important and what is not. Without inhibition, every time you wiggled your toe or opened your eyes, there would be an electrical storm in your brain of the same sort that causes an epileptic seizure.

For a long time it was believed that brain cells used only a few main neurotransmitters and that some of them were stimulators and others were inhibitors. Then, as methods were devised to detect smaller and smaller amounts of biochemicals, and even to isolate the receptors on the surface of nerve cells, dozens of other neurotransmitters were discovered. In fact, researchers now believe that eventually there may turn out to be hundreds of them. Some of these chemical messengers may have different effects on different types of cells. The same neurotransmitter may stimulate certain cells and inhibit others.

When a neuron "fires," that is, transmits an electrochemical message along its length from dendrite to axon, it works according to what scientists call an *all or nothing principle.* When a nerve cell is stimulated, either it does not fire at all or it fires full-strength, sending the nerve impulse all the way through the nerve fiber.

Whereas the neuron itself seems to work like a simple on-off switch, the synapses and neurotransmitters provide the fine tuning for the nerve networks. Whether the neuron will fire or not depends on whether the stimulation it received is strong enough. That in turn depends on what kind of neurotransmitter crossed the synapse, how much of it was released from the terminal branch of the preceding neuron in the chain, and how many different terminal branches (from the same or different neurons) were transmitting firing signals at the same time. Depending on how the neurons in the nerve network are interconnected, all these factors can combine to direct the nerve impulse along one pathway or another, or perhaps along a number of nerve paths simultaneously.

The combination of stimulators and inhibitors operating within the brain's wiring circuits provides a wealth of information that the brain can interpret. How do you know whether an ant is crawling on your toe or a big rock has just fallen on it? How can the brain direct a very delicate finger pressure, as when picking up a piece of paper without crumpling it, or a powerful clenching of the same fingers, as when cracking a nut without a nutcracker? The difference lies in how many neurons in a particular set are firing at the same time. A rock falling on your toe would stimulate many more neurons than the tiny feet of a crawling ant. The number and kinds of neurons that are firing give the brain the information it needs concerning the strength and nature of the message.

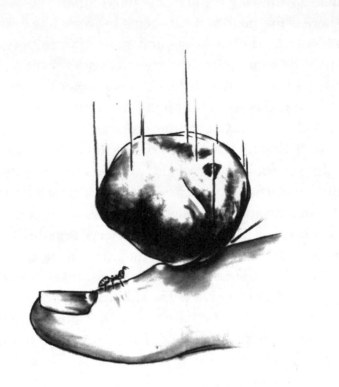

The brain works ceaselessly, even when you are sleeping, and it consumes prodigious amounts of energy. Although this organ accounts for only about 2% of the body's weight, it receives about 20% of the blood pumped by the heart. The brain regulates its own blood flow and can keep it fairly steady regardless of the blood pressure in the rest of the body. A reliable blood supply is essential because the blood carries food materials (a sugar called *glucose* is the brain's energy food) and the oxygen that is needed to release the chemical energy stored in glucose. If the flow of blood to the brain is interrupted for just ten seconds, a person loses consciousness; a four-minute interruption can permanently damage brain cells. Fortunately, the four arteries that carry blood to the brain are linked into an elaborate fail-safe system, so that if one or two of them are blocked, the blood can be rerouted through the others.

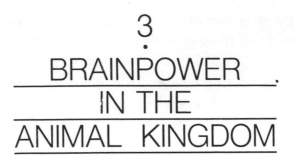

3

BRAINPOWER
IN THE
ANIMAL KINGDOM

Conscientious lawmakers sometimes wonder aloud whether some of the research projects that scientists work on are really worthwhile or just a waste of taxpayers' money. Indeed, to spend public money on a study of something like "Problem-Solving Behavior of the Lobster" might seem unnecessary or even a bit silly. Yet, in many areas of biology and especially in studies of the nervous system, research on animals can bring new knowledge and insights that can be applied directly to the human nervous system.

The basic principles of nerve structure and function are similar throughout the animal kingdom. (In fact, much of our basic knowledge of nerve action was acquired in studies of squids.) Although there are great differences in animals' brains, studies of the simpler brains of lower animals can help us to understand ourselves. The human brain, with its billions of nerve cells, is incredibly complex, but there are many animals whose brains are much smaller. A honeybee, for example, can gather nectar and pollen from flowers (a task including feats of navigation that humans can accomplish only with the aid of special tools), build and repair the hive, care for young, recognize and communicate with other members of the hive— all with a brain that contains only about seven thousand neurons. The roundworm *Ascaris*, which lives a much less demanding life as an intestinal parasite, still can learn, remember, and act on the basis of its observations using the brainpower provided by a mere 162 neurons.

In addition to being smaller than the human brain, the brains of lower animals show much less individual variation. For instance, a researcher can observe cell No. 56 in one lobster's brain, knowing that the 56th cell in the brain of another lobster will be in almost exactly the same place and have basically the same connections to other neurons. Also, working with a relatively simple brain like a lobster's, it is fairly easy to stimulate a particular cell with a microelectrode and know exactly which one is being stimulated.

Neurobiologists at Columbia University have been working with the marine snail *Aplysia* for more than two decades. They have discovered that this snail can learn and remember and that the learning process produces actual changes in the neurons of the brain: they release more of their neurotransmitter chemicals when they are presented with a new stimulus and less when the same stimulus is repeated. In one series of studies, the researchers investigated the snail's response to threats from the environment by withdrawing into its protective shell. In its relaxed state, the snail's gill extends out from its breathing chamber; but if the snail's body is touched, it quickly pulls in its gill. Yet, if the experimenters directed several harmless jets of water at the snail, its protective response was greatly reduced. The snail learned from experience that a particular kind of stimulus was not a threat and could be ignored. This learning behavior of a simple snail was similar in many ways to learning in humans. After just one training session, for example, the snail remembered its lessons for only an hour or so; if the training sessions were repeated several times, the change in the snail's response lasted for weeks. These differences in learning were very similar to the short-term and long-term memory observed in humans. For example, when you look up a new phone number, you usually can remember it just long enough to make the call; if you repeat the number over and over or call the same person frequently, you may remember the number for years without making any further effort.

Can studies of a snail's memory or the patterns of sleep and wakefulness in a cat really give us insights into the workings of the human brain? Indeed they can, for our brain is the product of a long process of evolution. It was built up from single neurons that were combined into groups and gradually specialized into various structures as increasingly complex animals appeared. Generally, instead of sweeping changes, new brain capacities developed by adding on new parts or expanding old ones. So the complex, multibillion-neuron brain of a human being today still contains parts that are very similar to the brains of our fish, reptile, and mammal ancestors.

Except for the single-celled creatures and some very simple animals such as sponges, nearly all members of the animal kingdom have a nervous system. The simplest animals possessing a structure that could be called a brain are the flatworms. *Planaria*, a typical example, is a tiny ribbonlike worm about the size of the tip of a fingernail. Planaria live in ponds, where they glide along the bottom or along the stems and leaves of pond plants on a ribbon of slime. They eat bits of decaying plant and animal life. If a planaria is cut in half, it will not die; instead, each half can grow back the missing parts and turn into a whole new flatworm. A planaria has an organized nervous system: a small "brain," which is a cluster of nerves in its head that relays messages from the worm's eyes and other sense organs, and two main nerve cords that run down its body and are linked together in a sort of ladder-like arrangement; but the flatworm's brain is not really the vital kind of organ that the human brain is. When a flatworm is cut in half, its rear half can move about quite normally without the control of a brain. In fact, some tests indicate that the brainless rear half "remembers" what the whole worm had learned before it was cut apart! Apparently both memory and the coordination of body activities are much less centralized than they are in the human nervous system.

The earthworm is a more highly organized animal than

the planaria, but even its brain is just a cluster of nerve cells grouped together. An earthworm, too, can live if its head is cut off. It doesn't act quite normally: it feeds slowly, moves rather awkwardly, and it is restless. Yet an earthworm without a brain can still learn its way through a maze. Eventually, like the flatworm, it can regrow a new head, complete with a new brain.

Among most of the other *invertebrates* (animals without backbones), the brain and other parts of the nervous system are not much more developed. You might expect that the most highly organized brains in the invertebrate world would be found in insects. The honeybee, remember, is capable of very complex behavior; and bees, ants, and some other insects can form smoothly running, well-coordinated "cities" in which the members cooperate to work for the good of the group. Actually, the typical insect brain is just a group of nerve masses, or *ganglia.* An insect's brain receives information from the sense organs of the insect's head and directs the body's movements, but its brain does not coordinate the actions of the body muscles. If a grasshopper's brain is removed, it can still walk and jump and even fly. In fact, it will jump or fly at the slightest touch or other stimulation. It seems, rather, that the insect's brain works to stop or inhibit any unnecessary movement.

Perhaps the largest and best developed brains among the invertebrates are those of the squids and octopuses. A squid's brain consists of several pairs of ganglia, all fused together. Several different centers of nervous control are

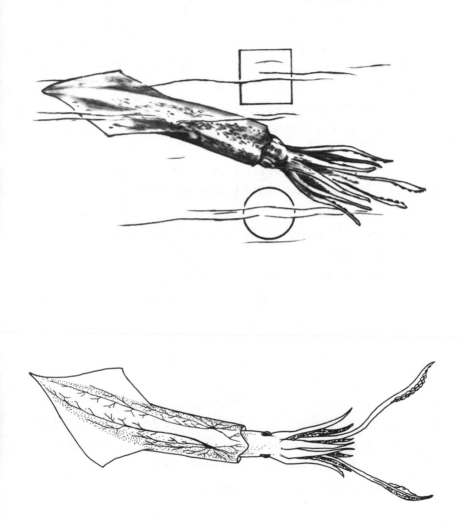

The squid's nervous system, though not very highly developed, permits some problem-solving behavior.

thus concentrated in one place in the squid's head instead of being spread out over its body as in most other invertebrates. Squids and octopuses have a pair of large eyes that work surprisingly like human eyes, and a large fraction of their brains is devoted to receiving and analyzing the sense messages from the eyes. Scientists who have studied octopuses found that they can be taught to solve simple problems. For example, an octopus learns rather quickly to choose between a circle and a square or between two circles of different sizes in order to get a food reward.

Although invertebrates do have a type of brain and can learn and remember to some degree, we do not find a brain that begins to resemble the human brain until we look at the *vertebrates* (animals with backbones). The vertebrate brain begins with a swelling at the head end of the spinal cord. This region is called the *medulla oblongata*. Then come various structures of the *midbrain*, the *cerebellum*, and the *cerebrum*.

A fish's brain looks quite different from a human brain. It is a long, hollow, narrow structure. The fish's medulla is quite large; many of the large nerves that go to various parts of the head are connected here. The cerebellum of a fish is also especially well developed, for this is the part of its brain that helps it to keep its balance as it swims through the water and controls the movements of its body muscles. Probably the most striking parts of the fish brain are the large *olfactory lobes*, which receive and process the information that comes in from the fish's organs

BRAIN POWER IN THE ANIMAL KINGDOM

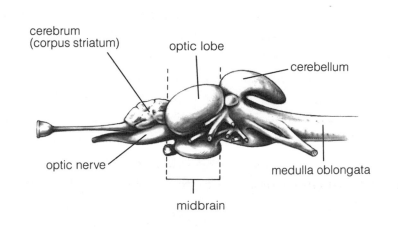

The fish brain. The cerebrum is relatively insignificant, and information is processed largely by the large optic and olfactory lobes.

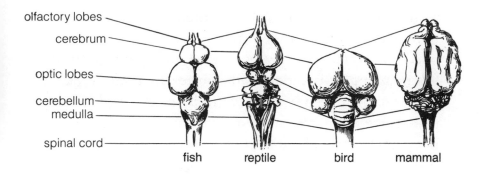

Development of the brain from fish to reptile, bird, and mammal shows a progressive increase in the size and complexity of the cerebrum.

of taste and smell, and the *optic lobes*, which process the messages from the fish's eyes. There is no real cerebrum, the structure that is the "thinking part" of the human brain. Yet, even without it, fish do have some ability to learn and remember.

In experiments sharks have been taught to tell the difference between horizontal and vertical lines and various shapes. Researchers who have worked with them believe that their "smell brain," the olfactory lobes, can handle more than just smell and taste information. They think that these lobes of sharks' brains work similarly to the human cerebrum, even though they are built differently.

The brain of a typical reptile, such as a turtle, begins to look a bit more like the human brain. Although there are large optic and olfactory lobes, the turtle's brain definitely has the beginnings of a cerebrum.

The humorous insult "birdbrain" doesn't really do justice to a bird's brainpower. Although it does not compare with a human's, the bird's brain is the most developed of all the vertebrates except mammals. A bird's brain is larger, broader, and shorter than the reptile's brain. A large, folded cerebellum helps the bird to keep its balance as it wheels and soars through the air in flight. Because a bird does not rely much on a sense of smell, the olfactory lobes are not very large. The optic lobes of the midbrain, on the contrary, are quite well developed: a bird must depend on its keen eyes to spot food and a safe landing place. A large part of the bulging cerebrum is involved also in receiving and processing information from

BRAIN POWER IN THE ANIMAL KINGDOM

the bird's eyes. With this bigger, better developed brain, birds show quite a degree of learning ability. Pigeons, for example, can be taught to pick out the odd item in a set. If a pigeon is shown two screws and a nut, it can learn to pick out the nut.

The most striking feature of the mammal's brain is the cerebrum. This "higher brain" receives and processes information both from the sense organs and from the more primitive parts of the brain. It controls and coordinates activities and is the conscious part of the brain, the part involved in thought and reasoning and decision making.

Going up the mammal family tree from our very dis-

The pigeon can master problems involving the oddity principle.

tant relatives, such as mice, to our closest relatives, the monkeys and apes, there is a clear increase in the size of the cerebrum. The brain of a mouse has a rather narrow, flattened, pointed cerebrum. A cat's cerebrum is larger and more rounded, and that of a chimpanzee far more so, although still proportionately less developed than the human cerebrum. The dolphin has a brain with just as large and prominent a cerebrum as the human brain. It also shares one of the most striking features of ours: the large number of folds, or *convolutions*, that greatly increase its surface area.

Generally, there seems to be a direct relationship between the amount of cerebrum and intelligence. Scientists who have studied animals' ability to learn to solve problems have concluded that cats are smarter than mice and that monkeys are far smarter than cats. Chimpanzees seem able to reason in an amazingly "human" way. They have been observed using tools both in the laboratory and living in the wild. For example, a chimpanzee offered a banana that is dangling out of reach may drag a chair over to reach it, pick up a stick to knock it down, or even fit two sticks together if one is not long enough. Chimpanzees living in the wild have been observed to carefully select and shape grass stems and twigs to fish termites out of their mounds.

A number of scientists have tried to teach chimpanzees to use words to communicate as humans do. The early attempts were failures, mainly because the researchers were trying to teach the chimps to speak, but these animals do not have the right kind of vocal cords to form and use words easily. Greater success was achieved when researchers tried to teach chimpanzees and other apes to communicate in other ways for which they do have the physical capacity.

Washoe, a chimpanzee raised like a human child by a couple at the University of Nevada, was taught to use symbols from the hand-gesture language of the deaf. Washoe not only learned the hand signs for many words, but she could also put them together into sentences. One of the combinations she invented for herself was "Give me tickle." (She loved to be tickled.) She called the refrigerator the "open food drink."

Another chimpanzee, Sarah, was trained at the University of Pennsylvania to "talk" using colored plastic shapes on a magnetic board. Each shape stood for a word or a concept (like "the same as"), and Sarah apparently was able to use them to ask and answer questions.

Since those pioneering studies, a number of other chimpanzees, as well as some gorillas and orangutans, have been taught to communicate either in American Sign Language or using plastic chips or keyboard symbols. Scientists still do not agree that these "talking" apes really use language in the same way that humans do, but some of their achievements are quite impressive. At the Gorilla Foundation south of San Francisco, a gorilla named Koko, with a sign-language vocabulary of more than six hundred words, asked for a pet kitten for her twelfth birthday. In the months that followed, people all

Chimpanzees and gorillas can learn to communicate by sign language or the manipulation of symbolic shapes.

over the world followed the story of Koko and her pet: She picked out a tailless Manx male kitten from a litter of three, named him "All Ball," and cared for him tenderly until he slipped out of the cage one day and was run

BRAIN POWER IN THE ANIMAL KINGDOM

over by a car. Koko cried when she was told (in verbal speech) that her kitten was dead, and her fans around the world waited anxiously for reports on her progress in finding a replacement. The first kitten she chose, another tailless Manx cat, turned out to prefer Koko's mate, Michael, who also had a sizable sign vocabulary and named the orange kitten "Banana."

Meanwhile, researchers at the Language Research Center near Atlanta are excited about the progress of Kanzi, a young pigmy chimp who learned to communicate with keyboard symbols by himself from watching while scientists taught his mother. Like Koko, Kanzi also seems able to understand a great deal of spoken English words and sentences.

The apes are the animals closest to humans, but another animal species also has shown signs of high intelligence: the dolphin. In their ocean home dolphins live together in large schools and cooperate to protect weak and sick members of their group. They seem to communicate with one another through a variety of clicks, squeaks, whistles, and barks. Scientists studying dolphin communication discovered that these mammals are able to master human language as well. They easily learn to understand spoken commands and to mimic many human words. Often dolphins also seem to understand some of the words they repeat. Studies of dolphins' speech and behavior are providing insights into a nonhuman intelligence that some scientists believe is second only to ours on planet Earth.

4
NEW WINDOWS
ON THE
BRAIN

An epilepsy patient lies on the operating table. A flap of his skull has been opened, and the surgeon, masked and gowned, bends over him, touching the living substance of his brain with a delicate electric probe. The patient is wide-awake, but he does not feel any pain because there are no sense receptors for pain in the brain itself. The doctor is looking for a tiny damaged region in the cerebral cortex that has been causing miniature electrical storms in the patient's brain. When the electrodes are touched to one portion of the brain, the patient says, "I see a bright light." In another area, the patient suddenly kicks with his foot. Another touch with the probe and the patient exclaims, "I hear my grandmother talking to me—but she died twenty years ago!" Suddenly, "There it is," the patient starts to exclaim, when he is caught by the violent seizure of an epileptic fit. The surgeon carefully destroys a tiny portion of the patient's brain, and the patient will be able to live out the rest of his life without fear of further epileptic attacks.

NEW WINDOWS ON THE BRAIN

Studies of epilepsy patients have revealed a great deal about the brain and what goes on in its various parts. Information has come, too, from people whose brains have been damaged by accidents or disease. Wars and automobile accidents in particular result in many head injuries. Doctors can match the part of the brain that has been injured to the types of things the patient can no longer do. Some brain-injured patients lose their ability to speak, to do arithmetic, or to move certain parts of their bodies. Some lose their memories, either completely or only certain kinds of memories, such as the memory of recent events or the ability to recognize familiar faces. Some seem undamaged, and yet it may be observed that their personality is somehow changed from what it was before. In one astonishing case, which occurred about a century ago, a four-foot-long iron rod was driven by an explosion through the front part of a man's brain. He not only lived for twenty years more, but he was able to go on working and earning a living with no loss of memory or thinking powers. Yet his friends all said he was no longer "the same man." Before the accident he had been quiet, polite, and efficient. Afterward he was stubborn and impatient; he cursed constantly, and he was always making wild plans and then giving them up.

Observations of the effects of brain damage or stimulation of the brain during surgery have provided a great deal of information about what parts of the brain control various actions and abilities. However, there are limits to how much these kinds of studies can reveal; moreover, they deal only with damaged or diseased brains, not with the workings of normal brains under everyday conditions. Experiments with animals have provided further information, but they, too, are of limited value, for no animal has a brain as complex and highly developed as the human brain. New methods of looking at the brain, without damaging it in the process, were needed.

The past decade or so has brought a number of exciting new ways of looking at the brain, each with its own kind of information to contribute. Computers are the keys to all these new tools and techniques. The combination of a computer with a viewing or measuring device yields a "smart machine" that can perform large numbers of measurements automatically, analyze the results, and display them in a vivid picture of contrasting shades or brilliant colors.

The first of the new scanners that are revolutionizing the study of the brain was the *CAT scanner*. It doesn't have anything to do with cats; its name is an abbreviation for *computerized axial tomography*. That is a technical way of saying that a CAT scanner uses a computer to build up a vivid image of a "slice" of a person's head or body. The picture is actually a composite of a large number of X-ray images produced by a narrow X-ray beam that travels in a circle around the long axis of a person's body. The machine that takes the picture is shaped like a huge doughnut; the patient, lying on a table, passes through the hole in the "doughnut."

Ordinary X-ray pictures are of very limited use in studying the brain. The image is formed by high-energy

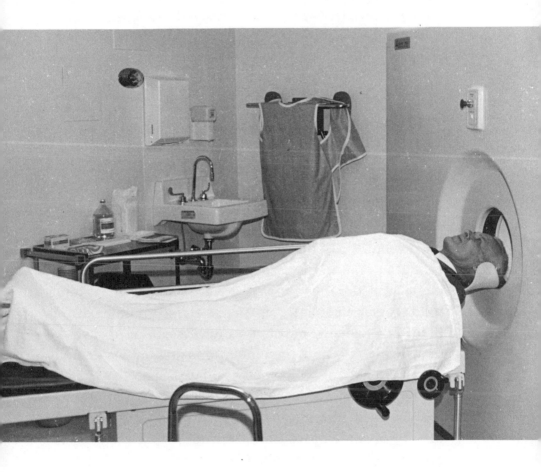

The CAT scanner.

X rays, which pass through soft tissues much more easily than through hard bone, so that the bones show up as shadows. But the brain is all soft tissue, and an ordinary X ray does not show the details of its internal structure.

Such X-ray pictures, however, can be used to detect a skull fracture that may have damaged the brain or to locate a bullet lodged in the brain. Doctors also can inject a special *radiopaque dye* (one that shows up on X-ray pictures) into the brain's blood vessels. Blockages of the brain's blood supply and *aneurysms* (balloonlike bulges in a blood vessel that might blow out suddenly, resulting in a stroke) can then be spotted on such X rays, called *angiograms.* An unusual concentration of blood vessels, which might be feeding a tumor, is another diagnostic clue that might show up on an angiogram. The contrast of a brain X ray also can be improved by injecting air into the fluid-filled ventricles of the brain. (Air provides a much greater contrast to the brain tissues than fluid does.) This technique, called *pneumoencephalography,* outlines the brain's solid masses and shows up any swellings or other distortions; but injecting substances into the brain can sometimes be risky, and pneumoencephalography generally leaves the patient with a colossal headache.

The advantage of a CAT scan is that the computer can analyze each image, amplify all the fine differences in density of the various brain structures, put them all together, and produce a detailed picture. Although a large number of images make up each CAT scan, the amount of X rays used to produce each one is much smaller than in conventional X rays, so the total exposure to radiation in the whole CAT scan is about the same as in a single X-ray picture of the conventional kind.

The first CAT scanners, introduced in 1972, were only

NEW WINDOWS ON THE BRAIN

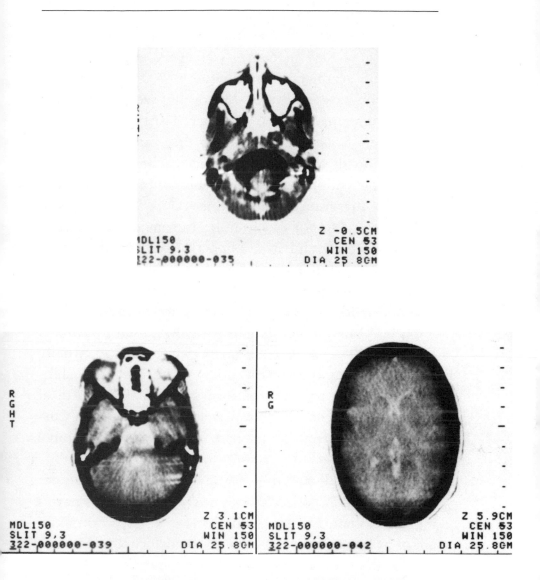

A series of CAT scans from different levels of the brain.

large enough to make images of a patient's head. Full body scanners were not available until a few years later. Although the new machines were very expensive—the early brain scanners cost about $350,000 each and the body scanners even more—the results were so exciting that hospitals rushed to order them. For head injuries, a doctor could use a CAT scan to find out if there was bleeding inside the brain and exactly where the damage was. People with headache problems could learn whether they were the result of a brain tumor or some other physical cause; if a tumor was found, surgeons could plan operations with confidence, knowing exactly where and how large the tumor was. In fact, the CAT scanner can be used during surgery to monitor the progress of the operation and guide the surgeon, helping to avoid damage to important brain structures. In many cases CAT scanners have made it possible to eliminate painful and potentially dangerous diagnostic procedures, such as pneumoencephalography and exploratory surgery. This medical tool has proved so valuable that its inventors, Allan Cormack and Godfrey Hounsfield, were awarded a Nobel Prize in 1979.

Even the small amounts of X rays that the CAT scanner sends through a patient's body carry some risk of harming the patient. Doctors would prefer to have no risk at all, or at least the smallest risk possible. That is one reason for the growing popularity of a newer kind of scanner, the *MRI device*. The letters stand for *magnetic resonance imaging*. The workings of this scanner are based on the

NEW WINDOWS ON THE BRAIN

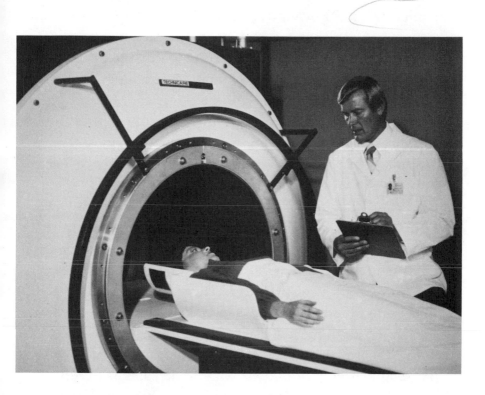

The MRI scanner.

effects that radio waves have on the nuclei of certain atoms. When "hit" by radio waves, they first line up like magnets and then act like tiny spinning tops that "wobble" in characteristic ways, sending out signals that can be picked up by a suitable receiving device. The intensity of the signals depend both on the type of atom and on its surroundings, so they contain structural information that a computer can use to build up a picture. This picture is similar to a CAT scan, but the MRI device does not send any radiations through the body. In fact, the medical community is currently trying to substitute the term MRI for an older name, NMR scanner, standing for *nuclear magnetic resonance*. It is thought that "nuclear" tends to be associated in people's minds with "radiations" and thus produces a misleading impression that might cause needless alarm. The radio waves that the MRI device uses have been shown to be harmless to body tissues.

In the MRI technique, hydrogen nuclei send out the strongest signals, and hydrogen atoms are very plentiful in the body. They are especially plentiful in water molecules; so the areas that show up strongest in MRI scans are those with a lot of water. These scans are good for observing blood flows and especially for picking out internal bleeding. (Blood plasma is more than 90% water.) MRI scans also can show tumors, because tumor cells apparently do not hold their water molecules as tightly as normal cells do. In one laboratory where researchers were testing a new MRI scanner, they were taking scans of people with brain tumors and blood-vessel disorders and comparing them with CAT scans. MRI devices pick up some tumors that do not show on CAT scans; for example, those at the base of the brain, an area overshadowed by bone on a CAT scan. They also show *plaques* (areas of hardened tissue that interfere with nerve function in multiple sclerosis) more clearly than CAT scans do; but they are not as good at picking up tumors with

NEW WINDOWS ON THE BRAIN

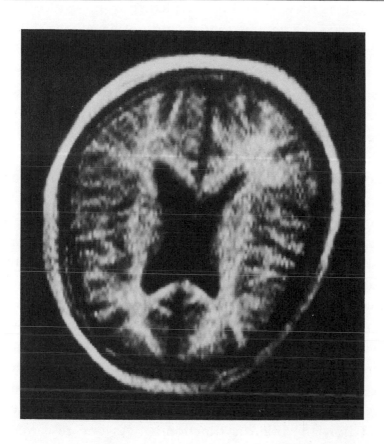

An MRI brain scan.

calcium deposits, which are imaged very well by a CAT scanner. A visitor to the lab asked to have an MRI scan done, just to see how it felt. The researchers assured the visitor that it wouldn't hurt, and he found that they were telling the truth; but he was surprised to hear them exclaiming as they looked at the picture of his brain. The scan showed something that should not have been there: a growth just behind the man's eye. Suddenly the visitor became a patient. He was sent for a CAT scan and other tests, which confirmed the results of the MRI scan: he had a brain tumor. When questioned by the doctors, he mentioned that he had been suffering from headaches for a while but hadn't thought they were anything serious. The tumor was removed by surgery, and after the operation the headaches disappeared.

MRI devices have some disadvantages. The scanners are very expensive (one to four million dollars each) and must be housed in a special part of the hospital, carefully shielded from FM and CB radios that might interfere with the radio waves used in the scans. The powerful magnetic fields that the MRI device uses can jam heart pacemakers and heat up the metal in artificial joints. There is another basic limitation that the MRI device shares with the CAT scanner: both of them produce pictures of the brain's structure, but they do not tell much about how the brain is functioning. As one researcher puts it, they produce "road maps without traffic."

Two newer approaches can show the "traffic," giving vivid pictures of the brain in action. One of these is the *PET scanner.* The letters stand for *positron emission tomography.* The PET scanner uses radiations, but instead of beaming them into the patient, it records tiny bursts of radiation coming from inside the patient's body. Before

NEW WINDOWS ON THE BRAIN

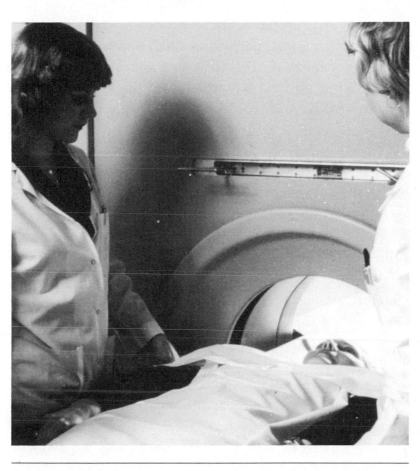

The PET scanner.

taking a PET scan, the patient is injected with a sugar solution "tagged" with a special radioactive substance. The
tagged sugar is carried in the bloodstream to various parts
of the body, and the cells take up and use the radioac-
tively tagged sugar in the same way as their normal en-

ergy food, glucose. Along the way, bits of the radioactive substance are constantly breaking down and producing ("emitting") minute particles called *positrons*. Positrons are very unstable. As soon as one meets an electron, the two particles combine explosively and shoot out a kind of radiation called *gamma rays*. Because all the atoms in our world contain electrons, a positron is destroyed almost as soon as it is made. (Having all those explosions going on inside a person's body sounds dangerous, but actually the amounts of radioactivity involved are too tiny to be harmful.) Gamma ray detectors can pick up the traces of positrons, and these traces are used by a computer to build up the picture in a PET scanner.

Like CAT and MRI scanners, the PET scanner provides a picture of the structures inside the body. It is also a functional picture, because its images show which structures are working most actively. Researchers can watch the "hot spots" on the vividly colored PET scans to see what parts of the brain are active when a person sees a light or listens to a voice or moves an arm or leg. Even thoughts, such as the decision to raise a hand, can show up on a PET scan. The PET scanner is also a powerful diagnostic tool for medicine. Scans have shown characteristic patterns of brain activity that distinguish various types of mental illness: in schizophrenia, for example, brain activity is abnormally low in the front part of the brain, whereas in patients in the manic phase of manic-depressive illness, brain cells in the same region are unusually active. PET scans show a striking decrease in the

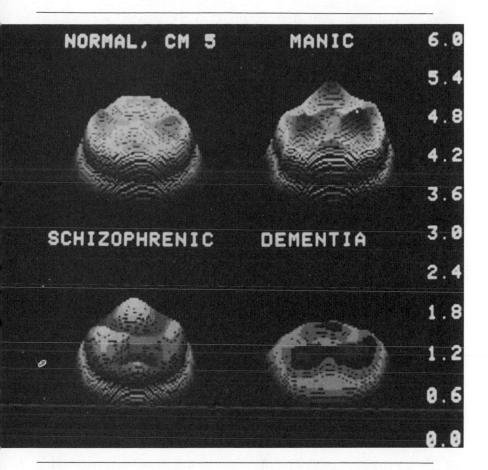

PET scans show strikingly different patterns of brain activity in various types of mental illness.

use of glucose in the side regions of the brain in patients with Alzheimer's disease, which is not observed in people who are suffering from high blood pressure or have merely become a bit forgetful in old age; the scans may make it possible to detect Alzheimer's disease in the early stages during which it could still be treated effectively with drugs to prevent further brain damage. Researchers are also working out ways to use PET scans to spot brain cancer in early, treatable stages. Other groups are mapping the distribution of receptors for various neurotransmitter chemicals in the brain and using them to learn more about various diseases. PET scans can pinpoint the abnormal area responsible for epileptic seizures and help surgeons to locate and destroy the faulty cells. They can also be used to predict how a person will react to various drugs and how much of a drug the person can take without suffering from harmful side effects. The main drawback to this versatile new device is its cost: a PET installation includes not only the computer and scanning device, but also a cyclotron to make the special radioactive sugar, and its total cost comes to several million dollars.

Another new "window" that is helping doctors and researchers to look at how the brain functions is actually a fairly old technique that has recently been revolutionized by the use of computers. This is the BEAM *machine (brain electrical activity mapping),* and it measures the faint bursts of electricity that come from inside the brain itself. (The amounts of electricity involved are so small that it would take sixty thousand brains to light up a flashlight.)

The electric currents flowing in the brain were first detected in 1875 by an English physiologist named Richard Caton. Like some later experimenters, he applied electrodes directly to the brains of animals, opening up their skulls in order to do it. In 1929 a German psychiatrist, Hans Berger, was the first to detect brain electricity with electrodes attached to the outside of the head, leaving the skull intact. Berger discovered four main rhythms to the brain's electrical activity. *Alpha waves*, which come at a frequency of 8–13 cycles per second, are observed when the mind is at rest. *Beta waves* (more than 13 cycles per second) are noted at times of conscious attention. *Theta waves* (4–8 cycles per second) are observed when a person is drowsy; and *delta waves* (fewer than 4 cycles per second) are characteristic of deep sleep. Since Berger's time great advances have been made in amplifying and interpreting brain waves by recording them on a device called an *electroencephalograph*. (The recording is an *electroencephalogram*, and both the machine and the recording are abbreviated as *EEG*.)

EEG tracings can provide a great deal of interesting and useful information. Characteristic patterns show if a person is a child or an adult, awake or asleep, thinking quietly or excited about something, or moving about actively. The electrical storm of an epileptic seizure can be traced on an EEG, as can the calmer course of a night's sleep. A glance at the paper tape unreeling from an EEG machine at a rate of about 350 feet per hour can tell a sleep researcher whether a sleeper is deeply asleep, about to awaken, or in the midst of a dream. EEGs also can help to discover and locate brain damage from a stroke, a head injury, or a brain tumor.

Researchers have been studying patterns of brain

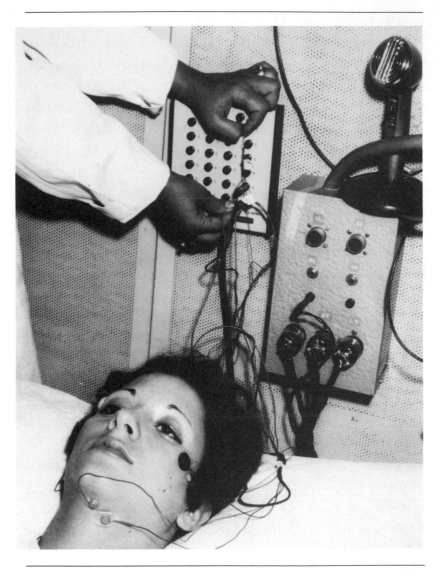

Pasted-on electrodes pick up the brain waves and movements of the facial muscles of a sleep-research subject.

waves to try to identify particular thoughts. Though they can't really read people's minds, they have discovered that there are typical patterns for certain kinds of thoughts. For example, a "surprise wave" appears on the EEG when something unexpected happens, such as the sudden ringing of a door bell. A different kind of brain wave appears when a person is concentrating on one voice in a crowd of people talking. (That particular brain wave gets smaller when the person drinks alcohol; he or she cannot concentrate as well.)

The EEG has also become part of the accepted definition of death in many states. In the past a person was considered dead if the heart stopped or if breathing ceased; but now techniques such as *CPR (cardiopulmonary resuscitation)* can be used to revive people whose hearts and breathing have stopped, literally bringing them back to life. Machines can be used to circulate the blood and send air into the lungs for people who cannot sustain these vital functions on their own. Such life-support measures can keep a person alive until surgery or some other treatment can repair the damage to the body; but they can also be used to maintain patients indefinitely in a sort of twilight zone of existence, long after any reasonable hope of recovery has gone. Transplants of hearts and other vital organs, taken from the body of someone who has just died and used to save the life of someone who is critically ill, have made ethical decisions of modern medicine even more complicated. With the old ideas of death no longer valid, reliable ways are needed to determine when a person is really dead, with no more hope of revival. It is becoming increasingly accepted that brain activity should be the basis for making such decisions: when brain activity has ceased, the person has died, even if breathing and heart action still are being maintained. A flat EEG (the absence of the typical brain waves) is used to determine "brain death."

The squiggly lines of EEG tracings can be very confusing, even for the experts. There is so much general "electrical noise" in the brain that it is often hard to pick out a particular event, especially when the researcher must go through yards of paper tape looking for items of interest. Various techniques have been devised to amplify the electrical signals and to pick out patterns that differ from the general background of "noise." Computers play a key role in sorting out EEG recordings and calling attention to significant patterns. A computerized EEG, for example, can amplify the electrical activity picked up by the electrodes about ten thousand times and pick out a hidden pattern with an amplitude of only a millionth of a volt. Using such devices, researchers can observe *evoked potentials* stimulated by a particular event, such as a picture flashed on a screen, a spoken word, or a thought.

The BEAM machine turns recordings of the brain's electricity into color-coded maps that, like the PET scans, are maps of brain activity. BEAM studies have proved valuable in diagnosing dyslexia, a brain abnormality that makes it difficult for a person to learn to read. Dyslexics typically reverse letters and syllables and tend

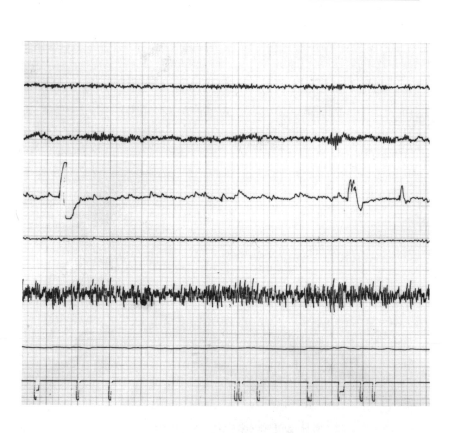

The EEG tracing shows the minute traces of electricity emitted by the brain.

to confuse pairs of letters like *b* and *d*. When dyslexia is not diagnosed early, children with the problem become frustrated and may regard themselves as stupid or bad; yet they may have normal or above-average intelligence, and with proper teaching they can overcome their handicap. (One dyslexic who became a superachiever was former Vice President Nelson Rockefeller.)

Patients suffering from schizophrenia show a characteristic abnormal pattern in a BEAM scan, and some abnormality persists even when the mental illness is not in an active phase and the person is outwardly normal. BEAM scan patterns can also be helpful in diagnosing other forms of mental illness, Alzheimer's disease, and epilepsy. In addition, researchers can use the BEAM machine to observe the activity in normal brains while people read, work puzzles, and do various everyday tasks. The BEAM scan allows researchers to follow the brain's activity while the action is going on.

With all the information that these new high-tech windows on the brain can provide, it may seem surprising that national and local government agencies actually have been purposely slowing down their introduction and use. The reason is their cost. A single scanner can cost from $800,000 for a BEAM machine and up to $4,000,000 for a sophisticated MRI installation. The high costs do not end there: the devices also need a support staff of highly qualified people to run them. The Congressional Office of Technology Assessment recently reported that nearly 30% of the increase in government Medicare payments between 1977 and 1982 was accounted for by technological devices like CAT and MRI scanners. Both government officials and consumer groups have asked whether the new high-tech instruments are worth the cost or merely a waste of money. Public health agencies stepped in and set strict limits on the number of hospitals permitted to buy and use the new scanners. Each application is considered individually, and many are refused. Even the prestigious Memorial Sloan-Kettering Cancer Center in New York was turned down when it first requested permission to install an MRI scanner, although the request was eventually approved. Yet many medical experts point out that not using the sophisticated new diagnostic devices is a foolish economy; in the long run the scanners can save both money and lives. Careful studies of the CAT scanners in use show that, in cases where a hospital is large enough to use the machine regularly, diagnostic costs to patients are lower because they make it possible to eliminate many other tests and shorten hospital stays. Often the use of a scanner makes it possible to avoid surgery. A $350 CAT scan, or even a $1,000 PET scan, is cheaper than brain surgery; and the scan carries practically no risk for the patient, whereas in any surgical operation there is a chance of damage or even death.

The dramatic advances in tools and techniques for studying the brain have resulted in some ethical dilemmas as well. Sometimes it is hard to decide what to do with the information that the scanners provide—or even to decide who should do the deciding.

BEAM scan studies suggest that it may be possible to identify schizophrenics even when they have no outward symptoms of the disease. If so, should we set up screening programs to identify potential schizophrenics? Once identified, should they be given treatment as a preventive measure, to protect them from possibly developing this mental illness? That might seem like a good idea; but virtually all drugs have side effects, and some of the best drugs used to treat mental illness can result in a serious condition called *tardive dyskinesia* when they are used for long periods of time. This condition is similar to Parkinson's disease, and its victims suffer from uncontrollable twitches and involuntary movements. In this particular case, the BEAM machine may provide its own solution by predicting how patients will react to the drugs and determining what doses will be safe to use.

Another set of brain wave studies has shown that there are characteristic patterns in the electrical activity of the brains of alcoholics and also their sons, even though the sons may not be alcoholics at that time. These findings suggest that a tendency to alcoholism is hereditary and also that brain wave studies may be able to identify people at risk. Should we have screening programs for alcoholism? Should they be compulsory? Who should pay for them? Should people who have been identified as alcoholic risks be held legally responsible if they drink and then cause a serious accident?

Early BEAM machine studies found abnormal brain wave patterns in the front part of the brain of a teenager who had been in trouble repeatedly for violent antisocial acts. This study suggests that it may be possible to identify young people with criminal tendencies before they have grown into hardened criminals. If so, should we set up screening programs for potential criminals? If we found them, what would we do with them? We do not know yet the best way to turn a juvenile delinquent into a law-abiding citizen. The various rehabilitation programs that have been tried work for some people but not for others. Do we have the right, in the interests of protecting society, to label certain young people as potential criminals when we do not know how to help them, or to take them into custody before they have committed a serious crime? The researcher involved in that early BEAM study, Dr. Frank Duffy at Harvard Medical School and Children's Hospital Medical Center in Boston, made his own ethical decision. He chose not to continue studies along that line, explaining that if he did find general brain-wave correlations with criminal tendencies, he would find himself being continually called to testify in court on whether or not young suspects should go to jail.

Like many important medical advances, the new tools and techniques for looking at the brain have raised some serious questions that do not have clear-cut answers. Nonetheless, the benefits these new devices offer in revealing new knowledge about ourselves and in providing powerful aids to medicine far outweigh these difficulties.

5
A GUIDED TOUR
OF THE BRAIN

What makes people act the way they do? What makes them eat, sleep, fall in love, raise children? What makes people angry and violent sometimes and kind and loving at other times? What makes them curious and eager to learn new things? What makes people love music and art? What makes them fight wars? These are some of the questions to which brain researchers are trying to find answers, and gradually they are unlocking some of the secrets hidden deep within the human brain.

Some scientists say that humans seem to have two brains, which are in a constant struggle with each other. One is the *old (ancient) brain*, the structures of the brain stem and the midbrain, which we inherited from our fish and reptile ancestors. The other is the *new brain*, the higher portions of the cerebrum, which began to develop extensively among the mammals and have reached their greatest development in humans. In the ancient brain are found the basic drives such as hunger and thirst and sex, along with various automatic controls of vital functions such as breathing. The new brain is responsible for conscious thought and decisions. If you feel hungry, for example, that is your ancient brain working. If you decide, however, that it would not be wise to eat a snack now because it would spoil your appetite for dinner later, that is your higher, new brain taking control.

Sometimes the ancient brain is called the "feeling brain," and the cerebrum is referred to as the "thinking brain." This seems to imply that all emotions come from the midbrain, and the cerebrum deals only with rational thoughts. Yet there are many interconnections among the various parts of the midbrain and the cerebrum, and they interact constantly. The higher brain is closely involved in our emotions. When you cry at a sad movie, this is certainly not an effect of your midbrain alone.

The first part of the brain, the *medulla oblongata*, grows right out of the spinal cord, and there is no obvious dividing line between them. A karate chop to the back of the neck can bring instant unconsciousness or even death by damaging the medulla, for this part of the brain houses centers that control breathing and the beating of the heart.

For a long time scientists believed that these were automatic functions, which could not be controlled consciously. Indeed, they named the parts of the nervous system involved in their control the *autonomic*, or independent, *nervous system*. There were stories of yogis and other religious mystics who claimed to be able to slow their breathing and even stop their heartbeat at will, but these were dismissed as trickery or exaggeration. Then scientists began to wonder if there might be something to such stories after all.

In the late 1950s researchers in India began to study yogis under controlled laboratory conditions. They soon found that these men could not really stop their hearts from beating, but they were able to slow down their heart rates to a surprising degree. In one experiment, a yogi was sealed in an airtight box. Electrodes and other pickups attached to his body made a continuous record of his heart rate, breathing rate, body temperature, and brain waves. Samples of air were taken from the box from time to time to determine how much oxygen he was using up and how much carbon dioxide he produced by breathing. The observing scientists calculated exactly how much oxygen the yogi's body would need to stay alive.

After the yogi was sealed in the box, his heartbeats and breathing rate gradually slowed. His oxygen consumption dropped down to the bare minimum—and then continued to fall! It plunged to only a quarter of the amount it was estimated he needed to remain alive. Yet when the yogi signaled a few hours later that the door of the box should be opened, he was alive and well.

In the United States another team of researchers was working with animals. Dogs were trained to control the amount of saliva that flowed into their mouths when they were offered a drink of water. Rats were trained to control their heart rate, blood pressure, contractions of their intestines, and rate of formation of urine—all functions that previously had been thought to be beyond conscious control.

Now doctors are applying the results of these studies through the techniques of biofeedback, which will be discussed more fully in Chapter 11. Heart patients can be taught to slow down their heart rate and lower their blood pressure. Headache sufferers can learn to relieve the pain of a migraine by draining blood away from swollen blood vessels in the head. Ulcer patients can learn to decrease the secretion of stomach acid. Meanwhile, researchers continue to explore these and other aspects of the mind's control over the body. They hope that such studies will reveal more about *psychosomatic diseases,* in which symptoms are caused by a patient's worries or anxieties rather than by a virus or bacteria or some other physical cause. (Psycho- comes from a word meaning mind; soma means body.) Researchers are learning that a person's mental state can have direct effects on the immune system, the body's defenses against invading viruses and bacteria and against cancer. Through such studies they hope to discover more about how people can harness their own mental powers and use them to help cure diseases.

In addition to the vital centers for breathing and heart rate, the medulla also contains control centers for swallowing and vomiting. The next time you are drinking a glass of water, try to stop swallowing once you have started. After a certain point, you will find that you cannot; the act of swallowing becomes automatic. Vomiting is also an automatic action, which may help to clear the stomach of irritating or poisonous substances.

Above the medulla the brain stem continues with another region, called the *pons*. Its name comes from a word meaning bridge, and it is a bridge between the spinal cord and the structures of the midbrain and 'tweenbrain, such as the thalamus and hypothalamus. It serves mainly as a relay station linking the medulla with the cerebral cortex.

Running up through the brain stem, from the medulla and pons into the thalamus and hypothalamus, is a cone-shaped network of neurons called the *reticular formation*. (Reticulum means net.) Unlike many other neurons, the nerve cells of the reticular formation tend to send out a continuous flow of impulses unless they are inhibited by signals from other parts of the brain. In experiments, if an animal's cerebrum is removed, there is nothing to stop the constant flow of impulses from its reticular formation. One effect is that the animal's muscles are in a constant state of stiffness because signals from the upper part of the reticular formation cause the body muscles to contract. Signals from the lower part of the reticular formation have the opposite effect, causing muscles to relax; so, if an animal's brain stem is cut across the middle, its body becomes limp. The stream of exciting impulses from the reticular formation helps to keep the body muscles in tone. Without them we would not be able to stand upright.

A GUIDED TOUR OF THE BRAIN

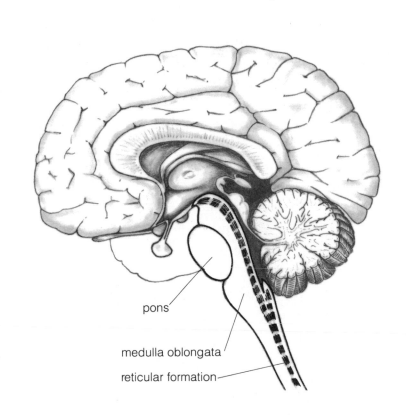
pons

medulla oblongata

reticular formation

The primitive brain contains many vital control centers for body functions.

The reticular formation has an even more important function. It houses the *reticular activating system*, or *RAS*. This is a sort of central clearinghouse for the flood of sense information that comes into the brain. The RAS determines which of the many bits of information are important enough—or novel enough—to report to the higher portions of the brain. You are conscious only of the information that your RAS allows your cerebrum to receive. Normally, the information relating to automatic actions, such as the heartbeat and digestion, is dealt with directly by the RAS, which sends out regulating impulses when they are needed without allowing any awareness of them to filter through to the conscious brain. It has been suggested that people who have learned to control their heart rate and blood pressure have found a way to let this information get through the channels of communication between the RAS and the higher brain.

Have you ever noticed that you can forget about some distraction, such as the loud noise of a pneumatic drill in the street outside, if you are very interested in something else—reading a good book or playing an exciting game? You no longer seem to hear the noise, even though it is just as loud and there is nothing wrong with your ears. Your RAS is blocking the sense information from your ears, permitting your conscious brain to concentrate on more interesting and important things. Without the ability of the RAS to block out some of the incoming information, the cerebrum would be swamped; it could not concentrate on anything in particular, and you would be thoroughly confused.

Minor aches and pains often seem unbearable at night, and small noises like the ticking of the clock seem more distracting then because the sense organs are not sending in as much other information. With less competition, the RAS sends these signals through to the higher brain, even though it might have blocked out the same signals during the day when you were busy seeing and hearing and thinking about other things.

The RAS does not consciously analyze or interpret the information that comes in. It does not "know" which kinds of signals to let through to the higher brain and which to block. It simply lets strong and unusual impulses go through, while blocking weak impulses and familiar patterns. In that way the cerebrum receives a constant flow of information about changes in the outer and inner worlds and then decides what to do about them.

There is a constant flow of messages back and forth between the RAS and the cerebrum. Stimulation by the RAS keeps you awake and alert; but when the flow of sense information and impulses from the higher brain drops below a certain level, the RAS shuts down the conscious mind and puts you to sleep. Do you have trouble going to sleep when you are very excited? Thoughts in your higher brain are keeping your RAS working overtime and preventing it from shutting down for the night.

Above the top of the brain stem is a pair of egg-shaped structures called the *thalamus*. This is the main relay station in the brain. Sensations from all the sense organs except sensations of smell are fed into the thalamus, which recognizes and analyzes the information and relays it on to the proper parts of the higher brain. In reptiles it seems that information about the world is perceived in the thalamus. In humans the thalamus provides only a crude sort of awareness, and real perception occurs in the *cerebral cortex* (the outer part of the higher brain).

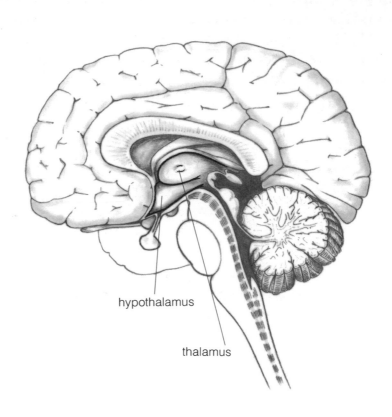

hypothalamus

thalamus

Structures of the 'tweenbrain help to screen incoming information and monitor and control body functions.

In front of the brain stem is another important structure, the *hypothalamus*. Together with the thalamus, it forms the 'tweenbrain (the part between the midbrain and the higher brain, or cerebrum). About the size of a pea and weighing only about one three-hundredth of the whole brain, the hypothalamus has an importance quite out of proportion to its size. By stimulating various parts of this structure with electric current and tiny amounts of chemicals, and by carefully destroying small portions of animals' brains and observing the effects, scientists have discovered that the hypothalamus acts as a central monitoring and control station in an amazing variety of the body's activities.

The hypothalamus works together with the autonomic nervous system to regulate various automatic functions in the body. Specialized areas of the hypothalamus receive information about the blood pressure and send out messages that help to adjust the blood pressure and heartbeat rate to meet the body's needs. If there is danger, the hypothalamus turns on the body's defense mechanisms. It makes the heart beat faster, sends more sugar into the blood (for energy), and increases the supply of the chemicals that make blood clot (in case you are injured and bleeding); it also stops the digestive processes to conserve energy for the muscles (in case you have to fight or run away).

As the body's "thermostat," the hypothalamus receives sense messages from heat receptors in the skin and also continuously monitors the temperature of the blood passing through it. If you are overheated, the hypothalamus makes the *capillaries* in your skin expand so your blood can be cooled faster, and it causes you to sweat and pant. If you are chilled, impulses from this control center in the brain make you shiver, producing heat by muscle action, and narrow the tiny blood vessels in the skin to cut down heat loss from the body surface.

Another control center in the hypothalamus acts as a sort of "appestat," regulating the amount of food you eat. Actually, there are two separate control centers: a *hunger center*, which stimulates eating, and a *satiety center*, which gives a sensation of fullness. A drop in the amount of glucose and other food materials in the blood triggers the hunger center; the satiety center responds to *hormones* (chemical messengers) that are released from the intestines while you are digesting the food from a meal. These natural controls do not seem to work properly in people who are chronically overweight. Studies have shown that obese people tend to overeat when foods are attractive and tempting but eat very little of foods that are unappetizing. They seem to be responding to impulses from the higher brain, linking foods with pleasant and unpleasant associations. In people of normal weight, on the other hand, eating behavior generally is governed by the body's needs, as determined by the hypothalamus.

The monitoring stations in the hypothalamus also keep watch over the blood to determine if the body is taking in enough water. If you are becoming dehydrated, a *thirst center* switches on and makes you want to drink water. Meanwhile, the hypothalamus produces a hormone called *vasopressin*, or *ADH*, that is sent through the blood to the kidneys and makes them conserve water, pouring out a more concentrated urine than usual.

The hypothalamus also contains a *sex center*. If an animal is stimulated in this part of the hypothalamus, it immediately becomes sexually excited; if a member of the opposite sex is present, it will attempt to mate with it.

Other hypothalamic control centers are concerned with emotions. Stimulation of the *fear center* in a cat's brain will make it cringe in apparent terror as a small mouse scurries across the floor of its cage. Stimulation of the *anger center* produces uncontrollable rage in which the pupils of the eyes widen, the heart pounds rapidly, the blood pressure rises, and the hair stands on end. One part of the hypothalamus is a *pain center*, and another—a large region that spreads from the front to the back of the hypothalamus—produces sensations of pure pleasure. In one series of experiments, rats were fitted with electrodes inserted in this *pleasure center*. (Electrodes implanted in animals' brains do not seem to hurt them or cause them any discomfort.) The rats were taught that if they pressed a lever, the pleasure center would be stimulated by a tiny electric current through the electrodes. The rats pressed the lever again and again. Some pressed it every two seconds for twenty-four hours without stopping. They ignored food even though they were hungry and went on pressing the pleasure lever until they fell down from exhaustion. A human volunteer in a similar situation pressed a button to stimulate his pleasure center three thousand times in ninety minutes! The experiment was stopped at that point by the watching researchers.

The various centers of the hypothalamus have been a main focus of studies of *electrical stimulation of the brain*, or *ESB*. Implanted electrodes have permitted scientists to control animals' moods and actions at will, and they have also permitted animals to stimulate their own pleasure centers or cut off stimulation of pain centers. In a classic series of experiments on a monkey colony, physiologist Jośe Delgado placed animals fitted with radio-controlled implanted electrodes together in social situations and studied their interactions. By pressing a button, Delgado could make a weak member of the group an aggressive leader or make the natural leader cower in fear. The monkeys even learned to press a lever attached to a radio transmitter when they wanted to calm down an angry member of their group.

Some people are alarmed by such studies. They imagine a future world in which everyone might be forced to wear implanted electrodes and submit to the will of a dictator who could control their moods with radio signals. Yet it is just as easy to imagine a future in which ESB is used to provide a safe and pleasurable means of amusement that would permit people to "turn on" without drugs through the power of their own minds. But would they have enough self-control to use the stimulators in moderation, or, like the volunteer who kept on stimulating his own pleasure center for an hour and a half until the experimenters cut off the current, would they lose themselves in mindless bliss, forgetting about eating, sleeping, working, and all the other necessary chores of life?

Actually, none of these science–fictionlike dreams—or nightmares—is likely to come true. Practical problems include the fact that the "wiring" of the neuron circuits in each person's brain is just as individual and unique as a set of fingerprints, and no two people have their control centers in exactly the same place in the hypothalamus. Moreover, the pleasure and pain centers are located just a fraction of a centimeter apart.

Nonetheless, some practical applications of ESB are being developed. In experiments with monkeys, researchers mapped about two hundred different points in the brain stem that controlled movements of various parts of the arms and legs. These maps were fed into a computer, which was then hooked up to electrodes implanted in the brain stem of a paralyzed monkey. Patterns of stimulation controlled by the computer permitted the monkey to feed itself, to climb, and to scratch its back. A set of switches permitted the monkey to control its own actions through the computer. Studies such as these are being used as the basis for developing brain pacemakers for humans that can send out electrical impulses that take over for a damaged control area in the brain. In a condition such as cerebral palsy, an electronic pacemaker would block faulty messages from the brain that make the muscles contract spastically; with the faulty transmissions inhibited, the person could move and walk more normally. ESB can also be used to relieve pain in diseases such as cancer.

The hypothalamus is connected by a stalk of nerves to the *pituitary gland,* one of the most important glands of the endocrine system. The pituitary is often called the "master gland" of the body, for its hormones control and regulate the work of the other endocrine glands, including the sex glands. In the past couple of decades, researchers have discovered that the pituitary, far from being a master, seems to be a servant of the brain. Its own master is the hypothalamus, which controls the secretions of the pituitary through a combination of nerve impulses and chemical "releasing hormones," which tell the pituitary when to send its secretions out into the bloodstream. In addition, two important hormones secreted by the pituitary gland are actually produced by the hypothalamus and are stored only temporarily in the pituitary. (One of them, ADH, or vasopressin, is the chemical messenger that helps the body to retain water when the monitoring centers in the hypothalamus show that more water is needed.)

Birth control pills, which women take to avoid becoming pregnant, actually work on the brain rather than directly on the sex organs. One of the many things that the hypothalamus constantly monitors is the level of sex hormones in the blood. When the levels of sex hormones in a woman's body are at a certain point, the hypothalamus normally stimulates the pituitary to secrete hormones that act on the sex organs to cause an *ovum*, or egg, to be released. This happens about once a month unless one of these ova is fertilized and the woman becomes pregnant. Birth control pills contain artificial sex hormones, which "fool" the hypothalamus into acting as though the woman is already pregnant. It does not signal the pituitary to release its hormones, and no ovum is released.

There is a constant interaction between the brain and the endocrine glands. Through the pituitary, the hypothalamus indirectly controls not only the sex glands, but also the growth and repair of the body and its smooth functioning under normal conditions and in emergency situations. The hormones in turn influence the brain. *Testosterone*, the male sex hormone, makes males aggressive and assertive. The cycle of female sex hormones secreted during the month seems to affect a woman's moods. Many women are irritable and depressed just before they menstruate. Some are more affected by this *premenstrual tension* than others, and studies show that women are more likely to commit crimes and suicide at this time of the month than they are at other times.

Scientists now believe that the monthly cycle in humans is regulated by another structure in the brain, the *pineal body,* or *pineal gland.* This small mass of nerves above the brain stem is shaped like a pinecone. For a long time the pineal gland was a mystery. In some animals, such as the frog, the pineal gland is located high up in the back of the head. It is sensitive to light and acts like a sort of "third eye." In humans, the pineal body is buried deep in the brain, but it has connections to the optic nerves that lead from the eyes to the brain. The pineal body receives messages through the eyes about the presence of light, and it is now thought to act as a timekeeper that helps to keep the cycles of the body in rhythm with the days and the seasons.

There are four little humps at the top of the brain stem, called the *superior* and *inferior colliculi*. They are all that remains in the human brain of the systems that process incoming information from the organs of sight and hearing in fish and reptiles. The superior colliculi are the remains of the optic lobes, and the inferior colliculi are relics of the sound analyzing system of lower animals. In humans most of the functions of these organs have been taken over by portions of the higher brain, the cerebral cortex. The colliculi remain as a sort of early warning system. The superior colliculi control reflex actions, such as blinking, the opening of the pupil, and the focus of the lens of the eye. The inferior colliculi adjust the ear to the amount of sound coming in and make you start at a loud noise.

Scientists have observed some curious things about the opening of the pupils. At first it was thought that this was a simple reflex, adjusting the size of the openings into the eye to take into account the amount of light available. (In dim light the pupils widen to let in as much light as possible; in bright light they narrow to cut down the glare.) Then a researcher noticed that he did not need as much light to read by if he was reading a particularly interesting book. He showed pictures of various things to people and watched their pupils. Sure enough, when they were particularly interested, their pupils widened, even though the amount of light was unchanged. The pupils of the young men tested widened when they were looking at a picture of a pretty girl, and the pupils of the women tested widened most when they were looking at a picture of a baby. If a person was shown a picture of something horrible, like an automobile crash, his or her pupils would first widen, then quickly narrow.

The thalamus, the hypothalamus, and other structures of the middle of the brain are linked together with parts of the cerebral cortex to form a looping network called the *limbic system*. The limbic system of the brain colors our thoughts with emotions. It helps us to recognize upsets, whether they are caused by basic drives such as hunger or sexual attraction, by dangers or threats, or by less tangible upsets, such as a broken promise or a worry about an upcoming test. Once the limbic system has given such upsets an emotional tag and the brain has recognized them, it can take steps to correct the problem and restore an equilibrium.

An important part of the limbic system is the *hippocampus*, a pair of structures shaped like bean pods. (To the imaginative anatomist who named it, the hippocampus looked more like a seahorse; that is the literal meaning of its name.) The hippocampus seems to be essential for forming long-term memories. A few patients have had the hippocampus damaged or removed because of disease. These people can remember everything that happened before the operation, but they cannot remember anything that happened afterward for more than a few minutes. A person without a hippocampus will forget your name within minutes after meeting you. Seeing you

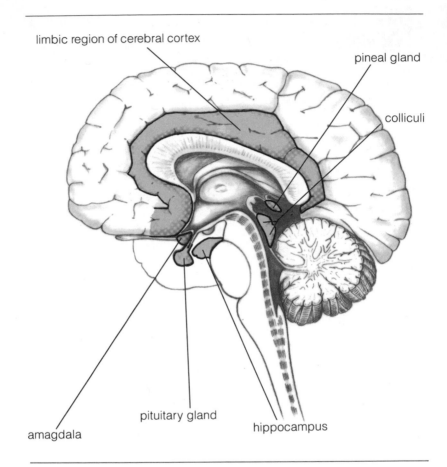

limbic region of cerebral cortex

pineal gland

colliculi

pituitary gland

amagdala

hippocampus

Structures of the limbic system are the seat of the emotions.

on the street on the following day, he or she will not recognize you at all. Such a person can read the same newspaper article over and over again and show new interest in it each time.

Another pair of limbic structures involved in forming memories is the *amygdala*. (Its name comes from a word meaning almond.) These small knoblike masses of nerve tissue have connections to all parts of the limbic system and also to the cerebral cortex, especially the parts involved in seeing and hearing. Experiences that arouse emotions are funneled through the amygdala to the rest of the limbic structures, especially to the hypothalamus. Stimulation of portions of the amygdala with electrodes can produce nearly all the same effects as stimulation of the hypothalamus, such as changes in the heart rate and blood pressure, effects on the digestive and urinary systems, secretion of various pituitary hormones, sexual activity, and even reactions of rage or fear. Stimulation can also cause various involuntary movements of the head or body.

Because of its connections with other parts of the brain, the amygdala has been called the "window" through which the limbic system sees a person's place in the world. It is thought that it helps to shape a person's behavior so that it will be appropriate to the situation. The amygdala and the hippocampus may aid in the formation of memories by giving information from the sense organs an emotional coloring. This information is then transmitted to the pleasure or pain centers in the hypothalamus, thus providing motivations for learning and remembering.

The limbic system provides animals with a set of *instincts* (automatic reactions to the information gathered by their senses). In humans the emotional promptings of the limbic system may clash with rational decisions made in the higher brain. Often we can deny or bury our feelings. For example, you can gradually overcome an "instinctive" fear of high places or of large animals. But sometimes the struggle between the limbic system and the higher brain can cause conflicts that are finally expressed in physical ailments, such as ulcers, skin rashes, and constant tiredness.

At the back of the brain, nestled between the cerebrum and the brain stem, is a structure called the *cerebellum*. If the cerebellum is stimulated with electric current, nothing in particular seems to happen. The person does not have any sensations, nor do any parts of the body move. Yet people whose cerebellums have been damaged by accident or disease cannot coordinate their movements properly. If they try to reach out to something, they reach too far before they can stop themselves. If they move an arm or leg very rapidly, they may lose track of exactly where it is. They find it difficult to keep their balance when they walk or run.

The cerebellum is the part of the brain that coordinates body movements. It receives a constant flow of messages from the body senses that tell it where all parts of the body are at all times. It knows whether they are moving and, if so, in what direction and how fast. The cerebellum is connected also with the *motor*, or movement-controlling, region of the cerebral cortex. It constantly receives information on what movements the higher brain (cerebrum) has ordered, and it compares these movements with the body's actual performance. If you are reaching too far for something, your cerebellum sends out mes-

A GUIDED TOUR OF THE BRAIN

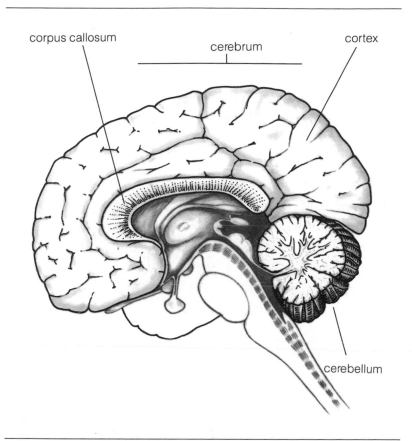

corpus callosum

cerebrum

cortex

cerebellum

The higher brain: the cerebrum is the "thinking brain," and the cerebellum coordinates body movements.

sages to stop some muscles from contracting and to cause muscles opposed to them to contract. So your movement slows down, and your hand winds up in exactly the right place. This correction occurs much quicker than it could if you had to think about it and send new messages from the cerebrum.

As you practice a physical action, you get better and

better at it. Your cerebellum is becoming more and more accurate in its corrections. For example, if you try to lift a heavy bucket of water up onto a table, you will raise it a bit too high the first time. But if you must lift one bucket after another, you will soon be doing it so smoothly that you could put the bucket right on the table with your eyes closed.

The structures of the primitive brain provide a good degree of awareness of the world and control over our actions. Indeed, many animals can live, get food, mate, raise their young, and even learn new solutions to problems with little more than just these brain structures. But for the thoughts and plans and dreams that make a human being truly human, we must look to the higher brain, the cerebrum.

Looking at the human brain, it seems astonishing that it could hold an uncountable number of facts, ideas, dreams—everything that makes a human being a person, a unique individual with experiences, desires, and hopes different from those of anyone else who has ever lived. Small enough to hold in your two hands, the living brain quivers like a gelatin mold, giving no hint of the storms of activity that go on inside it. The upper surface of the brain is rounded, fitting snugly inside the bowl-shaped skull. But it is not smooth. It is covered with a fantastic number of wrinkles and folds, ridges and furrows, spreading in a crazy quilt of irregular patterns. These folds or convolutions of the brain are more pronounced in humans than in any other animal. They are extremely important, as they help to increase the amount of information that can be crammed into the limited space inside the skull.

Spread out a sheet of newspaper large enough to cover a whole desktop. Now crumple it into a ball. It is small enough to fit into a teacup now, but not a single letter, not a single picture detail has been lost. A great deal of information has been stored in a much smaller space. This is exactly what the convoluted structure of the brain permits. Only instead of the thousands of letters on a newspaper page, the brain can store its information in special linkages among billions of microscopic neurons.

Most of the details on the brain maps that researchers have painstakingly compiled were obtained from the cerebral cortex, a thin outer layer that covers the cerebrum like the peel of an orange. It is generally said that the true thinking brain is actually this thin cortex rather than the whole cerebrum. Yet scientists believe that the vast "silent regions" beneath the cortex may one day yield their own exciting surprises.

The cerebrum is not one solid structure. Instead, it is neatly divided down the middle into two halves, or *hemispheres*, the left and the right. If you were to guess that each hemisphere of the brain is concerned mainly with one side of the body, you would be correct. But could you guess that the left hemisphere of the brain receives sense impressions from and controls the action of the right side of the body? And the right hemisphere, correspondingly, is concerned mainly with the left side of the body?

This curious circumstance is due to the fact that the nerves connecting the cerebral cortex with the rest of the body cross over to the opposite side as they enter the brain. Not only are the connections reversed in this way, but they are also upside down. The nerves linking the brain with the feet and the lower parts of the body have their connections near the top of the cerebral cortex; the nerves from the face and head are connected near the bottom of the cerebrum.

In addition to the crossover nerves connecting the cerebrum with the rest of the body, the two hemispheres are connected also at the bottom by a thick cable of nerves called the *corpus callosum.* This nerve connection permits each hemisphere to have a constant flow of information about what is happening in the other; thus, they can coordinate their activities.

The front part of the cerebrum (in the region of the forehead) is usually referred to as the *frontal lobes.* The back part (at the back of the head) is called the *occipital lobes.* The sides of the brain (near the temples) are called the *temporal lobes,* and the top part of the cerebrum (in the upper part of the head, toward the back) is called the *parietal lobes.*

In addition to the deep cleft that separates the two hemispheres of the brain, there are several other prominent folds and grooves, which are found in just about the same place in every human brain. One deep groove starts at the top of the brain, around the middle, and runs a zigzag course down each side. In front of this groove is a strip about an inch wide, called the *motor strip*. This part of the cerebral cortex has been mapped in great detail. If one part of the left motor strip is stimulated with a tiny electric current, for example, the person's right foot will suddenly kick out. Stimulating another part makes the right fist clench. The person does not have any feeling of wanting to clench the fist, and in fact may even try hard not to, but as soon as the electrode touches that point in the motor strip, the fist will clench.

You might expect the parts of the body to be represented along the motor strip in proportion to their size. However, only a small portion of the motor cortex is devoted to the legs and feet. A far larger portion of the motor strip controls the movements of the hands, and another large region is concerned with the face, particularly the lips, jaw, and tongue. On second thought, this seems quite logical. The hands and face perform a far greater variety of actions than the legs and feet, and far larger control regions in the brain are needed. So the representation on the motor strip is proportional not to the size of the body parts, but to their functions.

Next to the motor strip, in back of the deep groove, there is another strip of cerebral cortex that has been mapped in great detail. This is the *sensory strip*. When a portion of this strip is stimulated with an electrode, the person does not move any body parts. Instead, the stimulation results in a sensation as though someone were

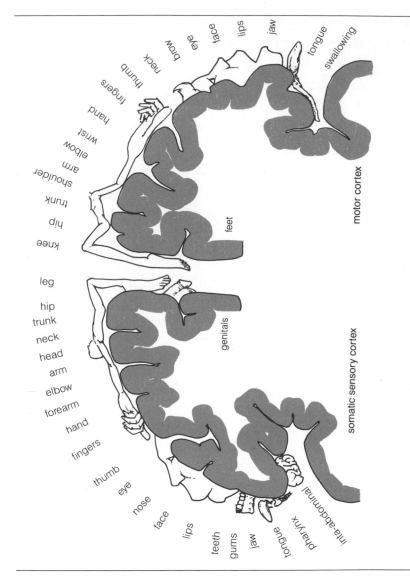

The sensory and motor strips: parts of the body are represented in proportion to their function rather than their size.

A GUIDED TOUR OF THE BRAIN

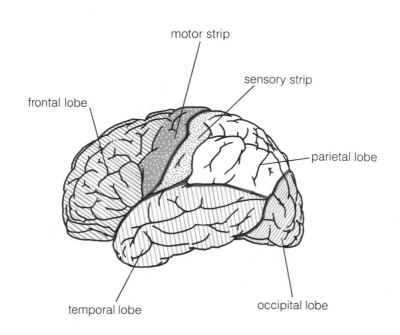

motor strip

sensory strip

frontal lobe

parietal lobe

temporal lobe

occipital lobe

The cerebral cortex is divided by deep indentations into four main lobes. (The brain is viewed from the side here, and only one of the hemispheres is shown. Compare with the top view on page 10.)

touching the person's back or hand or some other part of the body. As for the motor strip, there is a crisscross arrangement of nerves sending messages to the sensory strip: the cortex of the left hemisphere gets its information from the sense receptors in the right side of the body and vice versa. The arrangement of corresponding body parts along the sensory strip is very similar to that of the motor strip. Again, the representation of the hands and face is much greater than might have been expected.

Did you ever get a bump on the back of your head and "see stars"? It has been found that the visual centers of the cortex are at the back of the brain. If brain cells in this region are stimulated—by electric current or a bump on the head—the person may "see" flashes of light, even in a perfectly dark room. You may also "see stars" if you get a bump on the front of the head. What happened in that case is that the impact of the blow caused your brain to bounce back inside your skull, and the visual cortex in the occipital lobe banged against the bony cranium.

Some of the nerves that connect the retinas of the eyes with the visual centers of the brain cross over into the opposite hemisphere. Others, however, do not. Thus, the visual center in each hemisphere normally receives some information about what *both* eyes are seeing.

A variety of cells, both in the retina of the eye and in the brain, receive and process information about the intensity of light, shapes of objects, their movements, and so forth. In the visual areas of the brain, all these bits of information are put together, compared with past experiences, and meaningful patterns are found. So actually, although the eyes are the organs of vision and gather the visual sense information, you don't *see* anything until the information is processed in the visual area of the brain.

It's amazing how much the brain can do to make sense

out of the sensory messages from the eyes. For example, can you read this word: ʋɪ̸sɪ̸øɳ? Your brain is able to pick out the meaningful letters even when they are partly hidden by disguising lines. In an experiment volunteers wore spectacles with special inverting lenses. At first the volunteers groped and stumbled their way around, because everything they saw was upside down. After a while a curious thing happened. As the volunteers continued to wear their inverting glasses through all their waking hours, they suddenly realized they were seeing things right side up again. The lenses were still inverting what they saw, but now the brain had begun to invert the inverted images to see tables and chairs and other everyday objects the way past experience said they should be. When the volunteers took off the glasses, they saw the world upside down again and had to go through another period of adaptation while the visual cortex relearned which end was up.

Some curious optical illusions have been discovered. For example, which line seems longer:

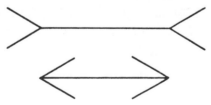

Now measure them.

In the picture on page 90, what do you see: black silhouettes of two people's faces or a white goblet? Do you find the picture switching back and forth from one to the

An optical illusion: do you see two faces or a goblet?

other? Can you make the switching stop and see just one or the other continuously? These and other optical illusions work because of the way the brain analyzes the information from the eyes, not because of what the eyes actually see.

Experiments using electrical stimulation and studies of people with brain damage have made it possible to draw up fairly detailed maps of the cerebral cortex, matching particular areas with the functions they appear to control. At each side of the brain, just below the sensory strip, there is an area involved in sensory messages from the ears. A large area in the parietal region is associated with hand skills. The frontal lobes are concerned with thoughts, plans, decision making, and various other aspects of personality. (Remember the man whose forehead

A GUIDED TOUR OF THE BRAIN

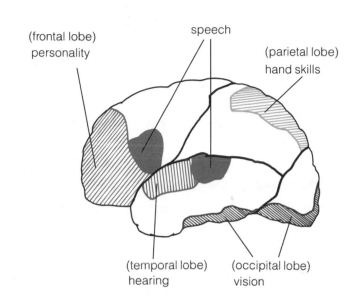

(frontal lobe)
personality

speech

(parietal lobe)
hand skills

(temporal lobe)
hearing

(occipital lobe)
vision

A brain map: the sites controlling various functions have been located on the cerebral cortex.

was pierced by an iron bar? There have been other cases of severe damage to the frontal lobes where the patient survived without any apparent loss of intelligence or skill, but experienced pronounced personality changes.) An extensive portion of the cortex on the underside of the temporal and occipital lobes is devoted to recognizing faces. Various *association areas* permit us to put together information from different sense receptors (for example, the sight of a baseball hurtling toward you and the "whooshing" sound of the air as it approaches) and to link sensory information with motor tasks. (In experiments on monkeys, if a particular association area is destroyed, the monkey still can see objects and still can move its hands, but it will no longer reach out for an object that it sees.)

Several different areas of the cerebral cortex relating to speech have been mapped. Speaking is a very complicated action, which includes such individual aspects as associating ideas, deciding on the words to be used, and actually forming the words. Strokes, head wounds, and other forms of damage to the brain can short-circuit one of these speech areas; as a result, the person is unable to speak intelligibly. The loss of the ability to speak is called *aphasia*. A person afflicted with aphasia may still be able to think quite well, and may even be able to write meaningful sentences; but efforts to speak bring only grunts or a stream of meaningless words and nonsense syllables.

It has been found that in right-handed people, the speech areas of the cortex are located in the left hemisphere of the brain. Many left-handed people have a speech center in the right hemisphere, but others have it in the left hemisphere, just as right-handers do; typically, speech and some other functions may be less *lateralized* (heavily concentrated in only one of the two sides of the brain) than they are in the average right-hander. Handedness, the dominance of one brain hemisphere over the other, and the division of functions between the two hemispheres have been the focus of a number of fascinating studies, which will be explored next.

6
LEFT BRAIN
RIGHT BRAIN

Most people tend to favor one hand over the other in daily tasks. They use this "dominant hand" to write, to eat, and to reach out for things. The other hand has its share of manipulating skills and participates equally in some activities, such as typewriting; but generally the dominant hand has greater dexterity and strength in tasks ranging from sewing on a button to drawing a picture to throwing a ball.

For the vast majority of the human population—about 90%—the dominant hand is the right hand. The other 10% or so favor the left hand. The degree of dominance varies: some people use one hand for writing, another for eating; or they may use one hand for most daily activities but bat or throw a baseball with the other. A small minority, who can use either hand with equal skill, are said to be *ambidextrous.*

It is still a mystery why humans tend to favor one hand over the other, a pattern that extends to other body parts, such as the foot and the eye. Even more mysterious is the origin of our overwhelming preference for the right hand. Studies of animals do not offer many clues. Most animals use either paw with equal ease; although left-pawed or right-pawed mice and cats have been observed, these species tend to have equal numbers favoring each hand. Our closest relatives, the monkeys and apes, show some tendency for handedness, but—by a narrow margin—the majority of them seem to be left-handed.

It is certain that handedness is controlled by the brain. In most people the left hemisphere of the brain is a little larger than the right, a difference that is present even at birth. Thus, the dominance of the right hand over the left is correlated with a greater development of the left hemisphere of the brain. (Remember, because of the crisscrossing of the nerve fibers leading to the brain, the left half of the cerebral cortex receives sense messages from and controls the right half of the body, and the right hemisphere is linked with the left half of the body.)

Heredity seems to play a role in determining handedness, but there is no simple relationship such as there is for the inheritance of eye color or the shape of the ears. Early training may change some lefties to righties, but another factor seems to be involved, too. Babies who suffered minor brain damage at birth are about twice as likely to be left-handed as the rest of the population. Doctors now believe that there are some "natural" left-handers, but others are natural right-handers who became left-handed because of an injury to the brain while it was developing.

LEFT BRAIN RIGHT BRAIN

During the 1860s and 1870s, a French neurologist, Paul Broca, and a German neurologist, Karl Wernicke, made some key discoveries about the brain. Studying people with brain damage, they found that when certain areas of the cerebral cortex were damaged, the person lost the ability to speak intelligibly. The areas that they discovered, which now bear their names, are associated with different aspects of speech. *Broca's area* is concerned with the ability to put syllables together to form meaningful words. People with damage to Broca's area can still make sounds, but they are able to say only very simple words, such as "yes" or "no." *Wernicke's area* controls the ability to understand and use symbolism; a person with damage to that area of the cortex loses not only the ability to speak, but also the ability to read, to perform mathematical calculations, and to understand the logical relationships between things. Both Broca and Wernicke noted that the ability to speak was lost when these characteristic areas in one hemisphere (in most cases the left) were damaged, but damage to exactly the same spots in the other hemisphere did not seem to have any effect on speech. In normal brains the speech areas were better developed on the dominant side. Thus, language ability seemed to be found in only one of the brain hemispheres and not in the other. Gradually, as new studies brought in more information, researchers concluded that there is a relationship between the dominant speech areas and the dominance of one hand over the other. Right-handed people would thus have their speech areas in the left half

WORLD OF THE BRAIN

of the brain, whereas left-handers would have dominant speech areas in the right brain.

Further studies revealed that the situation is not so simple. Although about 95% of right-handers have their speech areas in the left hemisphere, so do about 60% of left-handers. Only a small minority of left-handers show the expected left-hand/right-brain crisscross pattern. Many left-handers have the controls for speech abilities distributed between the two halves of the brain. So do some right-handers. In general, however, women tend to be less *lateralized* than men, with less concentration of certain types of speech abilities in one dominant hemisphere. Some researchers have suggested that competition between speech centers on both sides of the brain may explain why stuttering is more common among left-handers than among right-handers, who tend to be more lateralized. Yet girls (less lateralized) tend to develop verbal skills earlier than boys and continue to be more verbal at all ages. If a person has a stroke that damages one of the speech areas in the cerebral cortex, less lateralization makes it easier to regain the lost abilities.

Studies by a Japanese researcher, Tadanobu Tsunoda, in the 1970s have suggested that the language a person learns as a child determines how the brain control areas will develop. In the brains of right-handed Americans, Europeans, Koreans, Chinese, and Bengalis, speech sounds are processed by the left hemisphere; but animal sounds, music, and mechanical sounds such as bells, whistles, and helicopter noises are processed on the right side of the brain. Vowel sounds are a special case: they are processed on the right side if they occur alone (for instance, the *oo* sound) but in the left hemisphere if they are combined with consonants (*boot*, for example). The brains of Japanese and Polynesians process sounds differently. Vowels and consonants are both processed in the speech centers of the left brain, and animal sounds and Japanese music also are handled by the left hemisphere; only mechanical sounds and Western music are processed in the right brain. The explanation for this is probably that in both Japanese and Polynesian languages vowels often can occur by themselves as words, and Japanese music is designed to sound like the human voice. It is not a person's nationality that determines how sounds are processed in the brain, but rather the language the person learned to speak as a child. Japanese-Americans brought up speaking English have the typical Western lateralization, whereas Americans raised in Japan process vowels and other sounds on the "language side" of the brain, just as the native Japanese do. Bilingual people, who grow up speaking two languages fluently, have larger areas of the brain devoted to speech than people who speak only one language. That seems logical, as a person speaking two languages must be able to keep straight two different sets of vocabularies and sentence-structure rules and be able to retrieve the right word for each meaning from the two duplicate sets. Interestingly, the second language learned takes up a larger area in the cortex.

WORLD OF THE BRAIN

Information about how the two halves of the brain work has been obtained in a variety of ways. Observations of what is lost when the brain is damaged have led to some key discoveries; others have been made during surgery, when the surface of the brain can be stimulated with electrodes. Much of our knowledge of the brain hemispheres has come from studies of very special types of brain-damaged patients, the so-called *split-brain patients*. These are people who were suffering from severe epilepsy that could not be controlled by drugs or other usual treatments. "Electrical storms" spreading through the brain of an epileptic produce convulsions and unconsciousness. It has been found that surgically cutting the *corpus callosum*, the thick cord of some two hundred million nerve fibers that joins the two hemispheres, can stop the "electrical storms" from spreading and thus cut off the epileptic attacks before they can develop fully. In a normal brain there is a great deal of interchange of information from one side of the brain to the other through the nerve connections in the corpus callosum. In a person with a split brain, where these connections have been cut, there can be situations where truly "the left hand doesn't know what the right hand is doing."

Split-brain operations for severe epilepsy were begun in the late 1930s, and at first there did not seem to be any detectable effects—except, of course, the relief of the epilepsy. People with a split brain could still read and write and speak. They could walk, run, bicycle, and swim quite normally. Even with the nerve connections between the two halves of the brain cut, there is still plenty of opportunity for one hemisphere to find out the information that the other is receiving. The eyes in particular contribute a constant flow of information. Normally, each half of the brain receives sense information from both eyes. This is an exception to the general crossover wiring: the left hemisphere of the brain receives sense messages from the left half of the retina at the back of each eye and thus receives an image of everything in the *right* half of the field of vision. The right hemisphere is supplied by nerves coming from the right half of each retina, and thus it gets the information on the *left* half of what each eye "sees." The normal brain puts the two halves of the picture together, but if the corpus callosum is cut, each hemisphere "sees" only one side of the field of view (the opposite side). The split-brain patient is not aware that anything is wrong and sees a whole picture because the eyes move constantly, zigzagging back and forth, up and down, resting for a moment on one detail and then moving on to another. The eyes move so quickly that they soon cover the whole picture, and the brain automatically fills in any gaps.

In the 1960s Roger Sperry and his coworkers at California Institute of Technology devised a series of experiments to determine exactly what the two halves of the brain can know and do. (These experiments ultimately won Sperry a Nobel Prize.) In Sperry's experimental setup, a split-brain volunteer gazes at a spot in the middle of a screen while pictures are flashed quickly on the screen. These are very special pictures: Each is made up of two half pictures joined in the middle. On the right there may be half the face of an old man, while the left shows half the face of a child. The volunteer does not realize that there is anything unusual about the picture! If asked what the picture shows, she will reply, "An old man." But if asked to point to the picture she saw among a group of possible choices, she would pick out the picture of the child without hesitation.

In Sperry's experiments, split-brain patients did not notice anything unusual about pictures like this one.

LEFT BRAIN RIGHT BRAIN

In such experiments, the volunteer acts as though she had two separate brains, each with its own differing set of experiences and abilities. The volunteer's speech center is in her left brain; so when asked to tell what she saw, she tells about what she saw on the right. Her right hemisphere can guide the hands for pointing, and tests like this have shown that the right brain is better at recognizing faces than the dominant hemisphere. So she points to the picture that she saw on the left side.

In another kind of test, the volunteer feels with one hand behind a screen and picks up an object. If she is holding the object in her left hand, she cannot tell the experimenter what it is; her right brain cannot control speech, and her left brain cannot receive the necessary information. Yet if she is asked to draw a picture of what she felt, she can do so with her left hand.

Although the two cerebral hemispheres of a person's brain are separated by a split-brain operation, the brain is still connected at the brain stem. Tests indicate that facts are not transferred from one side of the brain to the other in this case, but emotions can be. For example, a split-brain volunteer looks at pictures of geometric shapes flashing on a screen. Suddenly a funny picture is flashed onto the left side of the screen. Only the speechless right hemisphere knows about the picture, but the volunteer begins to laugh. When he is asked why, he cannot tell, because his left brain does not know.

It might be objected that studies of split-brain patients may not tell us what the normal brain is like, as the patients had the operation because they were suffering from severe epilepsy and may have had some abnormalities to start with. However, other studies with normal people have basically confirmed the split-brain findings.

In one series of studies, the anesthetic sodium amytal was injected into the internal carotid arteries of volunteers. The *internal carotids* are the main arteries supplying blood to the brain, and each one services half of the brain. Thus, by sending an anesthetic into one of the brain hemispheres by way of its carotid artery, that half of the brain can be put to sleep while the other half is still functioning normally. When volunteers were injected with sodium amytal while they were singing a song, the result depended on which artery was being injected. If the left hemisphere was anesthetized, the person would suddenly forget the lyrics of the song but could still carry the tune. If the right hemisphere was anesthetized, the person could remember the lyrics but would lose all sense of melody and rhythm.

Another type of test that can be used to study the two halves of the brain in normal people is a variation of the tests used on split-brain patients. Psychologist Jerre Levy and other researchers have used a *tachistoscope* (a machine that flashes words or pictures very rapidly) to present very brief glimpses of pictures or symbols to either the right or the left visual fields, and thus to the opposite brain hemispheres. To find out which side of the brain is specialized for verbal abilities, a word or nonsense syllable is flashed on the right or left of the volunteer's vision.

LEFT BRAIN RIGHT BRAIN

The subject must report what syllable was flashed. To determine the side of the brain specialized for pictures and shapes, the tachistoscope flashes a picture of a dot inside a rectangular box. The subject must identify the position of the dot on a response card that shows twenty possible locations. In other variations the volunteer must identify or recognize faces, facial expressions of emotion, or line slopes. If a person replies more quickly and accurately to the verbal tests when they are shown on the right side, and to the visual tests when they are shown on the left side, then the person has the speech centers on the left side of the brain and the visual centers on the right side.

Another type of test presents two different sounds to a volunteer simultaneously, one to each ear. In a typical right-hander, the right ear (left hemisphere) is better at identifying nonsense syllables, and the left ear (right hemisphere) shows more skill at identifying other kinds of sounds, such as piano melodies or dog barks. (The Japanese experiments described earlier in the chapter used a variation of this technique.)

In recent years brain-wave studies and PET scans showing which parts of the brain were active while people were working various kinds of problems or engaged in mental or physical activities have contributed additional information. Gradually researchers have built up a picture of the two halves of the brain, each with its special abilities. In most people the left half of the brain is the dominant hemisphere. It contains the centers for speech and for understanding language. It is strong in orderly, analytical thinking. Thus, the left brain is not only highly verbal, but also good at complicated arithmetic and problem solving. The right brain does not have much verbal ability, although it can understand simple words and do simple arithmetic; but it is good at recognizing shapes and their relationships to one another and it has a strong artistic sense. The right brain is concerned with musical rhythm and melody as well. It can solve problems, too, but not the way the left brain does. Instead of taking problems step by step, the right brain sees the whole picture and takes leaps of insight and intuition. It is also the side of the brain with a sense of humor. People with right-brain damage have trouble getting the punch line of a joke. They simply don't understand why it is funny and instead tend to analyze the joke, criticizing small details that do not really matter. Recent studies, however, suggest that negative emotions such as disgust and sadness are centered in the right hemisphere. (In depressed people there is greater activity in the frontal portion of the right brain than in people who are not depressed.) Feelings of happiness seem to be localized in the left hemisphere.

Neuropsychologists Elkhonon Goldberg and Louis Costa see the right brain as a jack-of-all-trades, always ready to tackle new problems by trying one solution after another until it finds one that works. The left hemisphere, in their view, is a specialist, able to solve familiar problems quickly and efficiently using well-tested methods. The researchers point to recent discoveries about brain structure that support their views. The right hemisphere contains many long fibers that connect regions of the brain specialized for processing different kinds of information. Faced with a new problem, the right brain can thus draw on varied resources, combining them into novel approaches. The right hemisphere also contains more association areas that are capable of complex and sophisticated processing of information. The left brain, on the other hand, contains large numbers of short fibers that permit it to concentrate on processing familiar information in great detail.

A number of studies indicate that the right hemisphere is active in learning new tasks, but after they become familiar their processing is shifted over to the left brain. Most people use the right hemisphere to distinguish melodies, but professional musicians use the left brain for the same kind of task. People who are learning Morse code can understand very short messages using the left hemisphere, but when they are working out long code sequences, their right brain is active. Yet experienced telegraph operators can read a long and complicated message in Morse code using only the left hemisphere. The right brain, generally good at visual tasks, has a special area reserved for recognizing faces; but when a person sees and recognizes a very familiar face, it is the left brain that is active.

The two halves of the brain work together in all our activities, each contributing their own special skills and complementing each other. When you read a story, for example, your left hemisphere mentally translates the written words into sounds, and figures out the meanings of complex sentences. Meanwhile, the right brain is appreciating the humor and the emotional content, fitting the new events into the general story framework, and comparing the story with past experiences to bring out new meanings.

We have been speaking of the left hemisphere as the verbal, analytical brain and the right hemisphere as the side that specializes in visual information, music, humor, and insight; but that is the case only for the majority whose left brain is dominant. For those with a dominant right brain, everything is reversed.

In the course of her studies of brain dominance and handedness, Jerre Levy discovered a simple test for determining which side of a person's brain is dominant. You do not need any complicated equipment; it's a do-it-yourself test that requires only a pencil and a piece of paper.

Write a few words on the paper, using your normal writing hand, and watch your hand as it moves. Is the pencil point toward you or away from you? Is your hand below the line of writing, or is it curled up above it? People use two main writing techniques: straight and hooked. If you are a straight writer, you hold your hand below the line and your pencil points away from you. If you are a hooked writer, you curl your hand up over the line and hold the pencil pointing toward you. Many left-

LEFT BRAIN RIGHT BRAIN

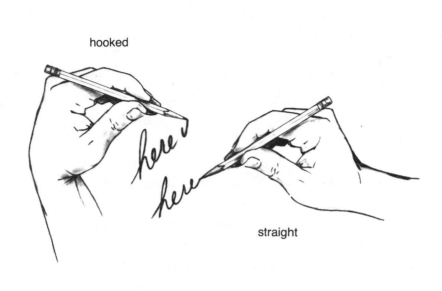

hooked

straight

A test for brain dominance: hooked writing and straight writing styles.

handers use the hooked writing style, and it was thought that they do this to get the writing hand out of the way so it won't smear the writing. But Jerre Levy found that the writing technique is actually determined by which side of the brain is dominant:

Straight right-handers have a dominant left brain.
Hooked left-handers also have a dominant left brain.
Straight left-handers have a dominant right brain.
Hooked right-handers also have a dominant right brain.

So only people (both right-handers and left-handers) who use the straight writing style have the normal crisscross relationship between dominant brain and dominant hand. The hooked-handers tend to have some of their speech and other abilities divided between the two halves of the brain.

With the current emphasis on studies of brain waves and other techniques to observe the normal, undamaged brain, it is ironic that new studies of brain damage have recently prompted some brain researchers to come full circle to the belief that the brain is not really quite as lateralized as it seemed. Sometimes, because of a spreading tumor or some major abnormality, it is necessary to remove a complete hemisphere of the brain to save the patient's life. It seems obvious what the results of such a drastic operation should be: because one side of the brain receives sense messages from and controls the actions of the opposite side of the body, removal of a hemisphere should result in complete paralysis of half of the body. Moreover, if the hemisphere that is removed was the dominant one, the person should lose the ability to speak; but doctors have been surprised to find that it does not work that way. After a time (much more quickly in children), the person begins to regain the lost functions. Somehow the remaining half of the brain takes over the jobs of the missing half. Even though the two hemispheres are normally specialized, each seems to retain the capacities of the whole brain.

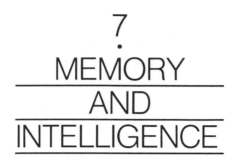

7
MEMORY
AND
INTELLIGENCE

What are the names of the people in your class? How many telephone numbers do you know by heart? Can you ride a bicycle? Swim? Can you name the players on your favorite baseball team and tell what positions they play?

Each day you learn hundreds of new things, even when you are not in school and even if you are not particularly trying to learn anything. The facts that you learn are stored away in your memory, and you may be able to call them to mind days, months, or even years later.

Just how do memory and learning work? This is something that brain researchers have been studying feverishly for years, and gradually they are discovering some answers.

First of all, there seem to be different kinds of memory. One distinction that can be made is between *fact memory* and *skill memory*. Your fact memory is filled with thousands of details—names, dates, telephone numbers, faces you can recognize, places you have visited or read about, historical events, and a great variety of other bits of information. These are the kinds of details that a victim of *amnesia* (loss of memory) cannot recall. Skill memories, on the other hand, are concerned with less conscious learning, which is acquired by repeated practice. Riding a bicycle, playing a musical instrument, using a typewriter, and working certain kinds of puzzles are examples of skill memory. Such memories persist for a long time, and if they are learned wrong, they are very hard to unlearn. If you have ever tried to correct your baseball or tennis swing, you can testify to that. Normally you do not recall a skill memory except when you are actually doing the action. Try to describe how to tie a shoe without actually "going through the motions," and you will find out how unconscious such a memory is. Trying to picture and describe each step becomes thoroughly confusing. Yet you can tie your shoes without looking at them or consciously thinking about the process, even while your mind is occupied with something else, such as watching television or talking to someone. People with damage to the hippocampus are unable to learn new facts. They can learn new skills, but they do not remember they have learned them. Such a person, for example, after being taught to work a particular kind of puzzle, can do the same puzzle with ease weeks or months later, protesting all the while that he or she has never seen anything like it before.

Learning facts seems to proceed in several stages, involving different kinds of memory. For example, look at this telephone number: 209-6622. Now cover the number with your finger. Can you still remember it? Probably you can, and you may even be able to picture the printed numbers clearly in your "mind's eye." But after you have read a few more paragraphs, or even a few more sentences, you will find that you have forgotten all or part of it. You may not even recognize it if you see it again. Yet you have no trouble remembering your own telephone number, and you probably know the numbers of friends, relatives, and perhaps some local businesses without having to look them up in the phone book each time you need them. If you move and get a new telephone number, you may find that you still recall the old one years later, although you no longer have any occasion to use it.

The first stage in the formation of a memory is a sort of photographic, or *iconic memory*. An image of something you have seen remains in your mind so clearly that if, for example, you look at a grid of numbers, you can actually close your eyes and read off the numbers in any row or column. When you watch a movie or TV, iconic memory fills in the gaps in the series of still pictures flashed on the screen so that they merge into a smooth-flowing "moving picture." In about a quarter of all children, this kind of photographic memory, precise in every detail, persists for long periods. Weeks after reading a page in a book, such a child can recall the whole page and read off the words. A few people retain this kind of photographic memory, but in most of us it gradually fades until, by the teen years, the image persists for only a fraction of a second.

WORLD OF THE BRAIN

Most of the images our minds perceive are discarded quickly. If they seem to have some kind of importance, they go into our *short-term memory*. When you look up an unfamiliar telephone number, for example, you can usually keep it in mind long enough to make the call. Studies have shown that the short-term memory has a very limited capacity: it can easily accommodate only about seven items. That is fine for such things as telephone numbers, unless you need to recall an unfamiliar area code in addition. Normally short-term memory lasts for about a minute.

Items that seem particularly interesting or important can be transferred from the short-term memory to the *long-term memory*. Several elements are necessary for that process. First, you must have some motivation to remember—either the prospect of some reward (an *A* on a test, perhaps) or the fear of a punishment. The next key element is repetition. If you repeat a new telephone number many times, you will be more likely to remember it later; and repetition is a good way to learn poems by heart. A third key to storing information in the long-term memory is association. If you can link a new fact with something you already know, you will have a much better chance of remembering it. The more associations it has, the more firmly it is fixed and the more easily it can be recalled later. People with unusually good memories commonly use a system of associations called *mnemonics.* For example, if you meet someone named Mr. Shoemaker, you might get a picture in your mind of a man making shoes.

MEMORY AND INTELLIGENCE

The picture then will serve as a mnemonic, or memory aid, that will help you to recall his name later. Rhymes make handy mnemonic tags: for example, "*i* before *e*, except after *c*" to help you recall a common spelling rule. A group of seemingly unrelated letters becomes easier to recall if you link them into a word or sentence: "Every Good Boy Does Fine" helps a music student remember the order of the notes on the staff, and beginning French students learn that "CaReFuL" holds the key to the consonants that are pronounced at the ends of words.

Can you remember the telephone number you read a few paragraphs ago? Perhaps you can recall the second part because you noticed that it contains two numbers, each repeated twice. Or perhaps you remember the first part because your own telephone number has a 20 in it. In each case fixing the memory was helped by associating the number with something else.

Studies have shown that facts and ideas are translated by the mind into language before they are stored in the memory, and words are stored the way they sound rather than the way they are spelled. Visual images seemed to be learned and remembered differently, and there is some evidence that they can pass directly from the iconic memory into the long-term memory, bypassing the short-term stage.

In one experiment a class of college students was shown a series of more than two thousand slides depicting people's faces and scenes. The slides were presented one after another, each shown for only two seconds. The next day the students were shown pairs of slides. In each pair, one slide was an image shown on the preceding day; the other was a picture the students had not seen before. When asked to tell which one of the pair they had already seen, the students scored 90% correct!

However, other studies have shown that eyewitness identifications are not always reliable. A victim of a crime may have only a few seconds' glimpse of the criminal, under very confusing, stressful conditions. Trying to recall the face later, the victim may confuse its features with those of other people or even unconsciously make up details in an effort to help the police. In one study volunteers were shown a film of a violent crime. The face of the criminal was never shown on the film, but when the viewers were asked to pick him out of a lineup of photos, 80% of them picked one. They "remembered" a face they had never seen. When this happens in real life, it can have tragic consequences. In 1979, for example, the city of Wilmington, Delaware, was plagued by a series of robberies by a man who was nicknamed the "gentleman bandit" because he was always polite to his victims. The police received an anonymous tip that he looked like a local parish priest. They put the priest in a lineup, and all of the victims identified him. Their testimony was so convincing that the police did not even bother to check out the priest's alibis for the crimes. He was arrested, brought to trial, and probably would have been convicted, as studies have shown that juries tend to give more weight to eyewitness testimony than to other kinds of evidence. Suddenly the trial was interrupted when another man, who looked a little like the priest, confessed to the crimes. His confession included details that only the actual criminal could have known; so the priest was freed, but he had suffered months of anxiety, was in debt from his legal expenses, and had lost the confidence of his parishioners.

How are memories formed and stored? How do we learn? How do we remember? There are still more questions than answers in this actively researched field, but gradually a picture is building up.

Researchers generally agree that memories are stored in the cerebral cortex, but other parts of the brain also are involved in their formation. Midbrain structures, such as the thalamus, hippocampus, and amygdala, play key roles in consolidating the fleeting images of iconic memories and the quick-fading traces of short-term memories into long-term memories that may last for a lifetime. The amygdala seems to be involved especially with emotion-laden memories, whereas the hippocampus is crucial in memories relating to places. Some researchers have suggested that the hippocampus works like a telephone switchboard, connecting distant parts of the cerebral cortex into a sort of "conference call" when a memory is first being created. But later, as the memory is reinforced by repetition or tied into associations with past experiences, connections between these parts of the cortex are established and they learn to "dial direct," bypassing the switchboard.

Exactly where in the cortex memories are stored is still

being debated. At one time it was thought that each memory had a very specific location on the map of the cortex. That was what the early studies seemed to imply: When a patient's brain is stimulated directly by electrodes during brain surgery, the patient may suddenly recall very clear and detailed pictures of past acquaintances, events, and places. There also has been a great deal of evidence that memories are actually distributed in many places over the cortex. In one series of experiments, rats were trained to run a maze, and then the researcher removed bits of cerebral cortex; but it did not seem to matter which part of the cortex was removed. The rats' ability to run the maze decreased in proportion to the amount of cortex that was removed, no matter from which part of the brain it had come. In another study monkeys were taught to open and close a latched box; then large portions of the cortex of their brains were removed. After the operation the monkeys' actions were slow, but they still remembered how to open and close the box. Brain-wave studies of cats in a learning situation showed activity over large areas of the cerebral cortex.

The new view of memory information as distributed widely over the cerebral cortex has been compared to a *hologram*. This is a sort of scrambled photographic recording that yields a vivid three-dimensional image when it is put into the appropriate decoding device. If a piece of the hologram is broken off and then unscrambled, it gives not a piece of the image, but instead gives an image of the whole picture, although the detail is not as sharp as in the original hologram. The smaller the fragment, the fuzzier the detail.

When a memory is formed, changes occur in the neurons of the cortex. In one series of experiments, rats were raised in three different situations. Rats from the same litter were used in each experiment so that there would not be any important differences due to heredity. Some of the rats were raised in a cage with an ample supply of food and water. Others were placed in separate cages. They, too, had as much food and water as they wanted, but they had nothing to stimulate their minds. The third group of rats was placed in an "enriched" learning situation. They were raised together in a large cage with food and water and several playthings, such as wheels to turn, sliding boards, and boxes to investigate. New toys were placed in the cage each day. After a while, all the rats were killed, and their brains were examined. The brains of the rats from the "enriched" environment were larger than those of either of the other two groups, and their cerebral cortex was particularly thick. The rats that were raised alone had the smallest brains and the thinnest cortexes. The increased brain size was due to two changes in the brain tissue: the dendrites of the neurons grew more branches, and the glial cells, which nourish and support the neurons, multiplied. The rats from the "enriched" environment also showed an increase in the neurotransmitter chemicals that carry the nerve impulse across the synapses between nerve cells. So did day-old chicks taught to avoid pecking on beads coated with a bitter substance. The synapses in the chicks' brains were 15% larger only one day after their training session. In a third study, rats were taught to run mazes while wearing a blindfold over one eye. Afterward, the side of the brain that "saw" the maze was found to have more highly branched neurons than the side that had not been stimulated.

There is still some debate about the nature of the changes in the neurons of the cortex and about how memories are stored. Studies in the late 1960s and early 1970s seemed to suggest that there is a kind of chemical coding of memories, and there may even be specific chemicals associated with particular memories. Hamsters were taught to go to a feeding box when a light was flashed, and then biochemicals called *RNA* (ribonucleic acid) were extracted from their brains and injected into rats. The rats then turned toward the feeding box when the light was flashed, even though they had not received any direct training. Other studies showed that when the brain is active, large amounts of RNA are formed. Old people whose memories were failing showed some improvement when they were injected with RNA or given drugs that stimulated the body's own RNA production.

In the body RNA directs the production of proteins, which do a variety of jobs in the cells. Experiments showed that protein production also plays a role in memory formation. In one series goldfish swimming in a tank were taught to jump over a hurdle in the middle of the tank to avoid getting an electric shock. If a drug that prevented protein manufacture was injected into a fish just after its training period, it seemed to forget its lessons. The next time it was placed in the tank, it ignored the warning light and got an electric shock. Yet, if the same drug was injected an hour after the training, the goldfish remembered what to do when the signal light went on. In that hour something happened to fix the lessons in the fish's memory.

Then a researcher reported he had isolated a certain proteinlike substance that seemed to act as a specific "memory chemical." The chemical was found in the brains of rats that had been trained to overcome their normal preference for dark places and run into a lighted box to avoid an electric shock. When this chemical (*scotophobin*) was injected into the brains of untrained rats, they, too, feared the dark. Later scotophobin was synthesized in the laboratory, and the synthetic version seemed to work not only on rats, but on mice and goldfish, too. Reporters speculated on the possibility of making chemical "memory pills," and students made jokes about turning cannibal and eating their professors to gain their knowledge. Gradually, however, reports came in from other experimenters who had tried to repeat the experiments and could not get the same results. Today most brain researchers believe that memory storage is electrical rather than chemical, in the form of circuits of neurons linked up in meaningful sequences.

When a neuron fires, its terminal branches release neurotransmitter chemicals that may stimulate other neurons to fire in turn. But there are literally thousands of choices for the next neuron in the sequence. What causes the nerve impulse to flow down one particular chain or net of neurons, and how does that electrochemical flow form a memory or trigger its recall?

Many researchers believe that temporary memories are maintained by a sort of *reverberating circuit,* a chain of neurons that continues to fire for a while after the original stimulus. Anything that disrupts the functioning of the brain, such as a hard blow on the head or a strong electric shock, stops the reverberations and instantly erases the temporary memories. Thus, a person suffering from a concussion after a blow on the head often cannot remember the events that occurred just before the accident. Even without a blow on the head, the reverberations in the neuron circuit will eventually die away unless something happens to change the neurons and make that particular sequence more likely to fire again.

The studies showing that RNA and proteins are produced during learning seem to fit together with the experiments in which the cortexes of animals in a stimulating environment grew thicker and the neurons of animals in a learning situation grew more branches. The new proteins could be part of the structure of the new neuron branches formed as memory circuits are established. But RNA and protein synthesis are processes too slow to account for the split-second fixation of iconic memories or even the consolidation of short-term memories into the long-term memory. Several groups of researchers believe that calcium ions hold the key to memory formation.

As you will recall, a nerve impulse travels down a neuron by a series of electrochemical reactions. At the terminal branches at the end of the axon, the electrochemical reactions stop, and neurotransmitter chemicals are released. These chemicals cross the gaps, or synapses, between the axon branches and the dendrites of other neurons. These dendrites are studded with numerous bumps, or spines, some of which hold receptors for the neurotransmitters. The chemical messengers then enter the dendrite spines and, if there is enough of the stimulating chemical, may spark a new series of electrochemical reactions that causes this neuron to fire in turn. Recently it has been discovered that calcium ions enter the dendrite spines along with the neurotransmitter. (Calcium is a mineral found plentifully in milk and bones, and it plays an important role in the contraction of muscles.) In the dendrite spines, calcium ions stimulate an enzyme that one group of researchers has named *calpain*. The enzyme sets off a chemical reaction that produces changes in the spine. The result is the formation of more receptors on the surface of the spine. So the next time neurotransmitters cross that particular synapse, the dendrite will take in more of these chemicals, and the stimulation will be stronger. Each time that particular neuron sequence fires, that pathway will get stronger, ultimately forming a new *memory trace*, or *engram*.

The individual memory traces in the brain are linked together into networks of associations. Each time one of

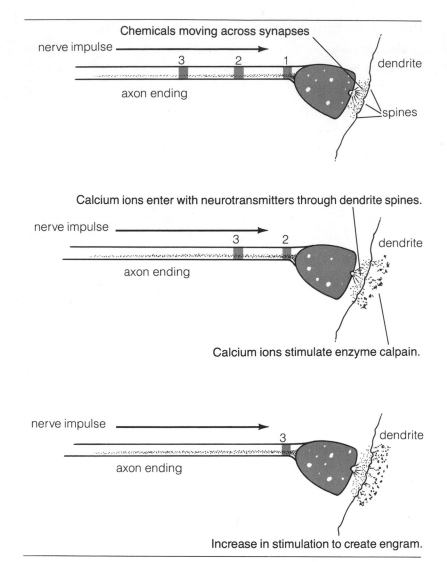

Chemicals moving across synapses

nerve impulse

3   2   1

axon ending

dendrite

spines

Calcium ions enter with neurotransmitters through dendrite spines.

nerve impulse

3   2

axon ending

dendrite

Calcium ions stimulate enzyme calpain.

nerve impulse

3

axon ending

dendrite

Increase in stimulation to create engram.

According to the current theories, a memory trace is formed when repeated stimulation of the same nerve pathways provokes the formation of more receptors for neurotransmitters.

them is triggered, it helps to strengthen the whole network, consolidating the memory and making it more easily retrievable. The memories in the brain seem to be organized into a complicated filing system that is full of "cross-references," any of which can trigger recall of the memory. Perhaps the smell of cookies baking in the oven reminds you of your grandmother. (Smells are especially strong memory triggers, probably because the sense of smell has the most direct nerve connections to the hippocampus and amygdala.) Once you have thought of your grandmother, not only can you almost "see" her face, but you can remember various things she said, presents she gave you, and so on. Scientists are not sure whether memories, once consolidated into long-term storage, remain in the brain permanently or whether some of them are gradually dropped out as new information is learned. We all have had many experiences of forgetting things that we once knew very well, but it is also a common occurrence to find that a name or fact you were trying unsuccessfully to remember suddenly pops into your head later. Or you may have no recollection of an incident—it is a total blank, as though it never happened—until a chance association triggers a memory, and suddenly the event is there in your mind in vivid detail.

Researchers are exploring various ways to improve failing memories. Some are practical techniques: for example, the use of mnemonics. Studies have shown that people remember things better not immediately after they have learned them but a few minutes later. This is called *reminiscence effect*. As a result, study sessions are more effective if you break them up with short periods of rest instead of cramming without a break. It has been found that you can remember things better if you can get into the mood you were in when you learned them. Certain foods and drugs may act as memory aids. A food substance called *choline*, found in foods such as egg yolks, meat, and fish, is one of the few biochemicals that can pass directly from the bloodstream into the brain. There it stimulates the production of *acetylcholine*, one of the main neurotransmitters. Researchers have found that choline food supplements produce some improvement of the memory of elderly people. Slightly changed versions of the hormone vasopressin, produced in the hypothalamus, also seem to be active memory stimulators and are now being tested on people with memory problems.

Memory and the ability to learn are a part of a complex set of abilities that we call *intelligence*. Other aspects of intelligence are the ability to solve problems, the ability to anticipate the results of actions, and various forms of creativity—putting together ideas or forms of artistic expression in new ways. Some people seem to have more natural ability to learn, remember, and solve problems than others. Scientists are still debating which is more important in determining intelligence: heredity or environment. It seems obvious that both play a role. Heredity determines the kind of brain you start out with; for instance, the number of neurons and their sensitivity to neurotransmitter chemicals. But environmental factors can shape the brain's development, especially during the crucial early years. Nutrition is very important. A child who does not receive enough protein in the diet during the early years may become mentally retarded for life. (That is the greatest tragedy in the great famines that have swept countries such as Ethiopia. Many starve to death, but among those who survive, a whole generation may be mentally stunted.) Later in life, after the brain has already been formed, a lack of B vitamins can interfere with effective functioning of the brain and thus make a person less intelligent. Studies have shown that a simple thing like eating breakfast in the morning can improve children's performance in schoolwork during the day.

You probably have already discovered that the more you use your brain, the more you learn, and the easier it is for you to learn. Each new fact and idea learned adds new associations that help in fixing other memories; and the more a skill is practiced, the more efficient it becomes. Experiments showing the growth of the cortex in young rats raised in a stimulating environment have helped to provide scientific support for attempts to provide enriched learning experiences for young children. "Head start" programs have shown promising results in increasing the knowledge and skills of disadvantaged children, although the "head start" is not always maintained if the intellectual stimulation is not continued in later years.

One problem in studying intelligence has been to find

tests that really measure intelligence. The first widely used IQ test was the Stanford-Binet test. It tests various kinds of abilities and skills: verbal and numerical skills, the ability to perceive spatial relations, and reasoning. The result is expressed as the *intelligence quotient*, or IQ, which is the child's mental age, as shown by the test, divided by the chronological age, and multiplied by 100 to get rid of inconvenient decimals. Thus, a ten-year-old who performed as well as the average twelve-year-old would have an IQ of $(12/10) \times 100 = 120$. Various other intelligence tests have been devised, and their scoring is somewhat more complicated, but they are generally designed so that about half of the people who take them score within the "average" range of 90 to 110.

The results of an IQ test may affect a child's whole life. The score determines whether teachers think of a student as "smart" or "dull." Experiments have demonstrated that a child often will act the way people expect, regardless of his or her real ability. In one instance, a teacher noticed numbers from 130 to 160 after the names of the students on the enrollment list for his class. Assuming that these were IQs and that he had been assigned a class of gifted students, he gave them more challenging assignments. He was not at all surprised when they responded by doing superior work—until he discovered a few months later that the numbers after their names were their locker numbers.

Many experts believe that the "intelligence tests" used today really do not measure mental ability; instead, they are gauges of what a child has learned. Children who have problems with the language or who do not identify with the culture of the majority of the country may appear less intelligent than they really are. Lack of motivation also can be a problem, as can poor nutrition or an upsetting home life that has placed the child under stress. Performance on IQ tests can vary greatly from one year to another, or even from day to day, which would not be the case if they were really measuring innate ability.

Devices that measure the speed of nerve action in the brain seem to be a better indicator of a person's intelligence. Wearing a helmet with electrodes that pick up brain waves, the person looks at a flashing light. A computer hooked up to the electrodes determines how long the brain takes to respond to the flashes by analyzing the brain waves. In most cases the results of the tests check well with the standard IQ tests; but in some cases children who had been classed as "slow learners" scored well on the tests of brain activity. These children were sent back to regular classes, and soon they were performing quite well.

One problem with all the tests and devices that attempt to measure intelligence is that it is a very complex combination of varied abilities and skills. The IQ tests currently in use are fairly good predictors of how well a child will do in school, but that is not necessarily an indication of later success in the adult world. The qualities that we value as "intelligence" in our culture may not be so useful in other cultures. As one researcher points out, a dyslexic, who has difficulties learning to read, is under a great handicap in our society and is considered to suffer from a "minimal brain dysfunction." Yet many dyslexics have superior artistic ability and other skills that could make them standouts in another kind of culture. Common sense, perseverance, and originality are qualities that intelligence tests do not measure, and yet they can be very important for success in life.

Questions of differences in intelligence between races or between the sexes are hotly debated and very emotional issues. On the average, blacks in America score lower on the standard IQ tests than whites; and Japanese have higher IQs on the average than Americans. In fact, not only are the averages higher, but at least 10% of the Japanese population has an IQ of 130 or more, whereas only 2% of Americans are in this category. Researchers cannot agree on whether these differences in scores mean anything in terms of real intelligence. Some have claimed that there are real differences, which are determined by heredity. Others argue that the apparent differences could be explained by cultural bias in the tests, differences in nutrition, and by the fact that IQ tests do not adequately measure all aspects of intelligence.

The same kinds of arguments are raging about sex differences in intelligence. The average woman has a somewhat smaller brain than the average man (probably because she has a smaller body), but there is no evidence of differences in overall intelligence between the sexes. However, there is some evidence that men and women

MEMORY AND INTELLIGENCE

are strong in different kinds of intelligence. Even before birth, differences can be detected in the brains of boys and girls: In girls the corpus callosum (the cord of nerves joining the two hemispheres) is larger, especially toward the back of the brain, where information about movements in space and about visual space is transmitted. From childhood, boys show an earlier development of the right hemisphere, which is concerned with *spatial* abilities (perceiving the shapes and relationships of objects) and mathematical ability. In girls the left hemisphere develops earlier; girls tend to be more fluent verbally and develop better fine muscle control. (Girls usually have better handwriting than boys of the same age.) As might be expected from the thicker corpus callosum, girls' brains are less lateralized, with control areas for speech and other activities in both hemispheres of the brain and a great deal of communication between them. Evidence is accumulating that all these differences are influenced by the effects of male sex hormones on the brain. These hormones apparently contribute to boys' higher math scores on standard tests, in addition to making them more aggressive.

Researchers emphasize that all these differences, both between races and between sexes, are only averages. There is much more variation *within* each group than between groups. The fact that there are so many great male writers is an indication that some men are far more verbally fluent than the average woman; and female athletic stars, with their superior spatial ability and muscle control, would make the average man look like a "klutz." Rather than using the results of IQ tests and research findings as labels to brand one group as "superior" and another as "inferior," it is far more sensible to treat each child as an individual and to try to develop his or her own abilities to the fullest.

Speaking of individual differences, there is a small and diverse group whose intellectual abilities are unique. These are the *idiot savants,* people who show extraordinary ability in one or a few mental skills, yet are ordinary or even below average in overall intelligence. Idiot savants can perform such feats as naming the day of the week correctly for any date within a hundred-year period, doing complicated arithmetic problems mentally, remembering whole pages of print after scanning them for a few seconds, or playing complex musical pieces after a single hearing. How they can perform at super-genius level in some areas while showing a rather poor level of intelligence in most others is one of the many mysteries of the brain that still remain to be solved.

8

EMOTIONS
AND THE
BRAIN

People give each other paper and candy hearts on Valentine's Day as a symbol of love, and we say that someone whose romance has just ended is suffering from a "broken heart." The word *courage* comes from a root meaning heart, and we are cautioned not to hold anger in our hearts. The heart is popularly viewed as the source of emotions. Yet scientists today know that this organ, although vitally important, is basically a pump that keeps blood circulating through the body. The keys to the emotions, from aggression and rage to tender feelings of love, are found in the brain.

National Institute of Mental Health (NIMH) researcher Paul MacLean says that we humans have a *triune*, or three-part brain. The first part is what he calls the *R-complex*, the structures of the upper brain stem and thalamus, which we have inherited from reptilian ancestors. In studies of animals as diverse as lizards, hamsters, turkeys, and monkeys, Dr. MacLean has found that the R-complex governs the behavior routines necessary for self-preservation and the preservation of the species. Feeding, grooming, and other day-to-day functions are controlled by the R-complex, as are the aggressive displays with which animals confront potential enemies, interact within their own communities, and court their mates. People with a severe form of epilepsy that short-circuits the connections between the higher and lower parts of the brain may show typical R-complex behavior, forgetting their learned fighting patterns and taking the stiff-legged, off-balance, arm-swinging stance typical of the aggressive displays of animals from lizards up to gorillas.

The second part of the triune brain is the limbic system, a heritage from our mammalian ancestors. The hypothalamus, amygdala, hippocampus, and other structures of the limbic system are concerned with the emotions that guide behavior. When part of the limbic system is destroyed, young mammals cease to play, and when they grow up, they can mate but do not care for their young properly.

The third part of the brain is the cerebral cortex, the thinking brain. Here are the keys to problem-solving skills and the ability to anticipate the consequences of actions in the future. The cortex is closely linked and interconnected with the other parts of the brain. Dr. MacLean believes that in the prefrontal cortex, which developed in close association with the limbic structures, family feelings and the bonds between parents and their young developed further into concern for other members of our

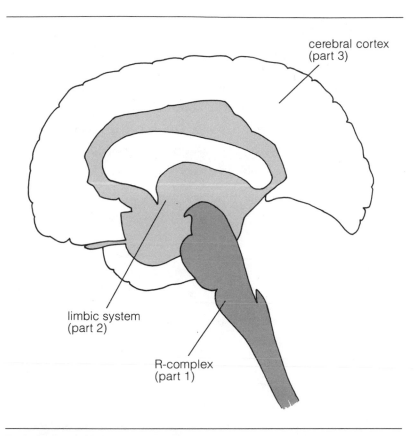

cerebral cortex
(part 3)

limbic system
(part 2)

R-complex
(part 1)

The triune brain: the three-part structure of the human brain is believed to reflect the development of our reptile and mammal ancestors.

species, and indeed for all living things. This part of the cortex is concerned with our sense of responsibility and the development of what we call "conscience."

A number of recent studies have focused on the brain's role in emotions. In one study two groups of juvenile offenders in a Connecticut reform school were compared:

those who had committed violent crimes such as rape, murder, and violent assault were compared to those who had been arrested for less violent crimes such as burglary or theft. Nearly half the violent group was found to have brain disorders, particularly damage affecting the limbic system, compared to only 7% in the nonviolent group. Brain tumors can cause violent, aggressive behavior. (Mass murderer Charles Whitman, who climbed to the top of a tower in Austin, Texas, and began shooting at passersby, killing seventeen of them, was found to be suffering from a brain tumor.) Alcohol and mind-altering drugs such as angel dust, or PCP (phencyclidine), also can lead to violent behavior. They act by dulling the higher parts of the brain that normally permit people to think about the consequences of their actions. Under the influence of alcohol or drugs, controls on behavior from the higher brain are relaxed, and the more primitive, reptile-like lower brain takes over.

Studies of brain chemistry have shown that certain neurotransmitters belonging to a chemical class called amines are at a low level just before aggression begins and then rise as aggressive behavior is acted out. Some doctors report success in treating violent patients with the drug *propranolol,* which blocks the action of some amines and prevents rage. In prisons, violent offenders with a hair-trigger temper, who fly into rages at the slightest insult or threat, have been brought under control with treatments of *lithium,* a drug that is also used to treat the manic-depressive form of mental illness.

EMOTIONS AND THE BRAIN

There seem to be two kinds of aggressive behavior: *defensive aggression* (a trapped animal will lash out with teeth and claws to defend itself) and *offensive aggression* directed against a perceived threat (such as the aggressive displays and violent attacks of an animal confronting an intruder in its territory). Heat, overcrowding, loud noises, and other conditions that increase the stress level can make aggressive behavior more likely. (Riots occur more often in the heat of the summer.) Punishment is not an effective way to stop defensive aggression, because it increases the pain, fear, and general stress level. Studies have shown that children who are beaten and abused by their parents are more likely to be violent and aggressive themselves when they become adults. Offensive attacks typically occur when people feel their rights are being violated. But brain damage, hormonal imbalance, or other abnormalities can distort a person's perceptions, so that trivial incidents are seen as major threats. (A prisoner may fly into a rage and severely beat another inmate who accidentally stepped on his toe; or a husband might attack his wife with a kitchen knife because she burned his toast.) In such cases the higher brain controls fail to operate, and the person acts without thinking.

Males are more likely to be aggressive than females, and high levels of aggression tend to be correlated with high levels of male sex hormones. There is some evidence that aggressive behavior is inherited: several studies of adoptees have shown that a much higher percentage of them become criminals if their biological parents had been convicted of crimes. Even the type of crime—violent crimes versus property crimes—seems to be influenced by heredity. These findings pertain to the sons of criminals; daughters do not usually follow the pattern, but women from violence-prone families frequently suffer from physical or psychiatric ailments.

Environmental factors, such as stressful living conditions and especially nutrition, also can influence violent behavior. In a sensational murder case a few years ago, the confessed killer offered a defense based on the assertion that his mind had become disordered from eating junk food. Sugar-filled snacks can stimulate the pancreas to secrete more of its hormone, *insulin,* which sends sugar out of the blood and into storage in the liver. If the pancreas overreacts, the sugar level in the blood may drop too low to provide the brain with the nourishment it needs. Theoretically, this could interfere with the workings of the higher brain and let the more primitive R-complex take over. Whether or not that is a valid defense in a murder trial, studies have shown that good nutrition can make a dramatic difference in behavior. When fruit juices were substituted for soft drinks and nutritious snacks were provided instead of high-sugar junk foods, violent behavior among inmates of fourteen juvenile institutions dropped by nearly 50%.

Whether the causes are hereditary or environmental, studies have shown that in many cases young violent offenders show differences in brain-wave patterns and in brain chemistry. These findings suggest that it might be

EMOTIONS AND THE BRAIN

possible to identify potential violent offenders at an early age, before they have committed serious crimes. If that is so, what should we do about them? One brain researcher recently stirred up a storm of controversy when he suggested that juvenile delinquents should be tested at the time of their first offense, and the potential repeat offenders (who account for at least half of all crimes in the United States) should be identified and trained to channel their aggressive tendencies into socially useful jobs. (One study has shown that some of these people make excellent deep-sea divers; the police and military professions also provide opportunities for aggressive, risk-taking personalities.) This seems like a socially desirable goal, but defenders of civil liberties object that this kind of information could be abused too easily. So far, at least, predictions of future violent behavior are only about one-third accurate.

Turning to the gentler emotions, brain researchers have also been studying the biology, chemistry, and psychology of love. The hypothalamus, with its sexual center, and other parts of the limbic system are involved in the intensely emotional sensations of falling in love. These emotions produce physical effects in the body: the heart rate speeds up, levels of lactic acid in the blood drop (making a person feel less tired and more energetic), and levels of endorphins (brain chemicals that produce a natural "high" and feelings of well-being) increase. Germ-fighting white blood cells become more effective, so that a person in love feels better and is actually healthier.

Studies have shown that people in love have unusually high levels of a brain neurotransmitter called *beta-phenylethylamine*. This chemical has amphetaminelike effects, promoting feelings of euphoria and boundless energy. When a love affair breaks up, beta-phenylethylamine levels fall, and the person plunges into depression. Often a jilted lover binges on chocolate, which seems to be a way of satisfying an unconscious urge: Chocolate contains large amounts of beta-phenylethylamine, which helps to replace the supplies of the brain chemical to which the person was accustomed. Some people seem to be beta-phenylethylamine "junkies" and fall into a pattern of plunging into one unsuitable love affair after another, with a wild seesawing of emotions. The victims are usually women, and doctors suspect that these women have some sort of disorder in their brain chemistry. Their craving for the druglike effects of their own brain secretions may prevent them from developing more long-lasting but less emotionally stimulating love relationships.

The stimulating effects of romantic love on the body's immune system and general well-being are just one example of the effects of emotions on the body. It has been known for a long time that stress, working through the brain, can give rise to various kinds of *psychosomatic illness* (actual physical ailments produced by interactions between the brain and the body systems). This mind-body connection operates through the hypothalamus via the pituitary gland and the autonomic nervous system. These two backup systems, hormone and nerve, produce a variety of effects on the body: raising the blood pressure; triggering the release of endorphins in the brain, which dulls the sensitivity to pain; and suppressing the responses of the white blood cells and other body defenses against disease germs and foreign substances. Ailments such as peptic ulcers, insomnia, spasms of the esophagus, and constipation or diarrhea may result from exposure to stress. Stress-provoked high blood pressure can contribute to the development of heart disease, and stress can also lower the body's defenses against cancer. Studies have shown that the death of a spouse or some other close family member, the loss of a job, and other high-stress experiences can make people more vulnerable to all kinds of diseases and may even lead to death. It is not uncommon for an elderly person to just "give up and die" shortly after losing a husband or wife, and the mind-body link appears to be the cause of death in primitive societies when a person has been placed under a "curse."

Stress is not always bad for the body; in fact, in some circumstances it can act to tone up the body and strengthen its defenses. The key factor seems to be a sense of being able to control the situation—or a feeling of hope. Young rats who were taught to stop or avoid a stressful electric shock by pressing a lever were much less likely to develop cancer in later life than rats who received similar shocks but had no way to avoid them. Some studies have shown that cancer patients with an active, positive outlook stand a better chance to survive than those who passively accept their condition with feelings of hopelessness.

In 1976 the *New England Journal of Medicine* featured an article by writer Norman Cousins titled "Anatomy of an Illness," in which he told how he had worked actively to recover from a serious case of spinal arthritis by adopting a positive mental attitude, laughing a lot (he watched slapstick movies for an hour a day), and taking vitamin C. The article brought an enthusiastic response from doctors, and Cousins wrote a best-selling book about his experience. That book and a later one called *The Healing Heart*, in which Cousins told about using a positive mental attitude to help his recovery from a heart attack, sparked a new way of looking at medicine and a search for ways to harness the brain's potential for healing the body. The study of the effects of emotions on the *immune system* (the body's system of defenses against disease) was christened *psychoneuroimmunology*, and reports on studies of the brain-body connection in illness and health began to appear. Cancer patients were urged to picture their white blood cells victoriously battling against the villainous cancer cells, and a video game called "Killer T-Cell" was devised as a psychological aid. Medical personnel were advised to be careful about saying negative things in front of patients, even patients under anesthesia or in a coma who may be able to hear and remember although they seem to have no conscious awareness; and some surgeons are trying positive suggestions as an aid in speeding their patients' recovery from operations.

Recently some medical researchers, calling such ideas "folklore," have challenged the idea that negative attitudes can contribute to disease and positive ones can aid in recovery. They point to studies that do not support such findings and claim that the emphasis on personality factors in disease may prompt some patients with serious diseases to rely on "mental attitude" instead of seeking the medical treatments they need; or patients may be caused needless suffering by making them feel that falling ill was somehow "their own fault."

Further studies should help to resolve such controversies and cast more light on the nature of our emotions and their effects on the body.

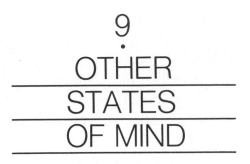

9
OTHER
STATES
OF MIND

It is midnight. Around the city, people are preparing for bed or already sound asleep. In the small laboratory room, a volunteer is also sleeping. He is lying in a bed with electrodes pasted to his forehead, his temples, and other parts of his head. They lead to a trailing crown of wires connected to a panel at the head of the bed. In the office next door, researchers rub their sleepy eyes, sip mugs of coffee, and glance back and forth from the sleeping volunteer to a moving ribbon of paper spilling out onto the table from an EEG machine that is tracing rows and rows of wiggly lines. Tonight while you are asleep, in dozens of laboratories around the world, researchers will be studying this fascinating state.

What happens inside your brain while you are asleep? You will spend about a third of your life in the sleeping state. Yet, from the time you close your eyes at night until you open them in the morning, you really are not consciously aware that anything is happening at all. Perhaps

OTHER STATES OF MIND

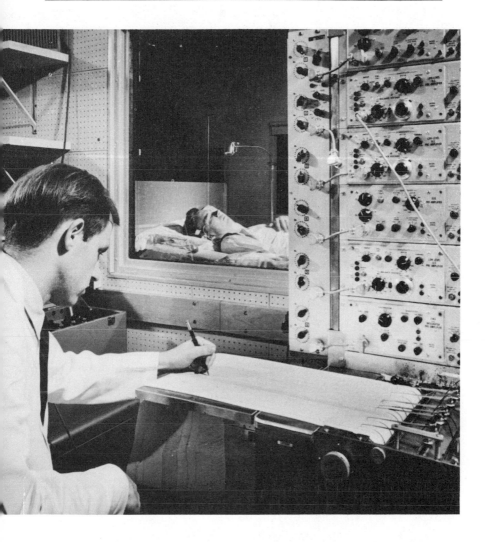

In a sleep research lab: the sleeper's brain waves will be recorded on about half a mile of EEG tracings in the course of the night.

you remember a dream you had, but the memory probably is not too clear, and the rest of the night is a complete blank.

Sleep researchers have found that the mind is far from blank during sleep. In fact, in some parts of sleep, the brain seems even more active than when it is awake.

As you are first settling down to sleep, an EEG machine recording your brain electricity would trace a wavelike pattern of alpha waves, indicating a mind at rest. Gradually EEG recording settles down into a pattern of big, slow waves. These are delta waves, and you are now in a state of deep sleep. Your body is completely relaxed, and even a loud noise probably would not wake you.

Then, after a while, the waves get faster. You seem to be rising into a lighter sleep. Yet you are not waking up. You are beginning to dream. The waves on the EEG are very fast now, and an observer can see that your eyes are moving rapidly back and forth under your closed eyelids, as though you were watching something. If someone woke you right now, you could tell exactly what you were dreaming about; but, if you were not awakened until the dream was over, you probably would not remember it.

The first dream of the night may last only a few minutes. Then the sleeper passes up into a lighter sleep, and then down again into a deep sleep, another dream, and so on, up and down, through the night. The cycles of deep sleep and of dreaming sleep, or *REM sleep* (named for the *r*apid *e*ye *m*ovements that occur during this stage), repeat

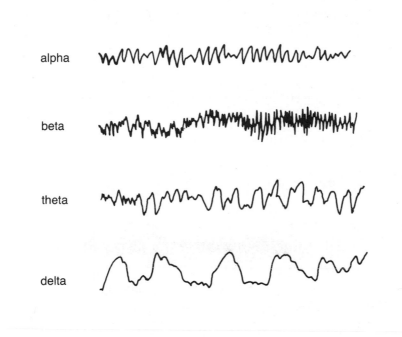

alpha

beta

theta

delta

Brain waves form characteristic patterns in different phases of sleep and wakefulness.

themselves approximately every hour and a half. As the night passes, the dreams get longer and more vivid, and the periods of deep sleep become briefer. Finally you awake, perhaps with a wisp of a dream memory to puzzle over.

Have you ever tried to keep from going to sleep all night? It is easier to stay awake if you have something interesting to do. Even so, as it gets farther past your normal bedtime, waves of tiredness wash over you, and they are hard to resist. Some volunteers have managed to stay awake for more than a week, but they soon became tired and irritable. After a few days, they even began to have hallucinations, seeing and hearing things that were not there.

What makes people sleep, even if they would prefer to stay awake? Studies of human volunteers have yielded much information, and so have studies of animals, particularly of cats, for many animals sleep in very much the same way humans do.

These studies have shown that a number of different systems in the brain work together to control the states of sleep and wakefulness. One important link is the *reticular activating system*, or *RAS*. This network of nerves in the brain stem can keep you awake by relaying a constant flow of signals from the sense organs up to the cerebral cortex. A neurotransmitter called *norepinephrine*, or *noradrenaline*, acts as a sort of natural "pep drug" that helps to keep the brain stimulated. Lights and noises and people moving around you can keep your RAS active and prevent you from going to sleep. Even busy thoughts or worries in your "thinking brain" are sent down to the RAS and can stimulate a flow of nerve impulses back up to the higher brain that keep you awake.

What causes the RAS to shut down for the night? It has been suggested that a "sleep hormone" is produced and accumulates during the waking hours, or that waste products of the body's chemical reactions attack the brain and bring on a state of sleep. A sleep center in the hypothalamus seems to be involved in the natural "turn-off switch" for the RAS.

A structure in the brain stem called the *raphe system*, located behind the RAS, is important in the sleeping state. The neurotransmitter *serotonin* helps in its work. (Do you usually drink a glass of milk before you go to bed? Milk contains large amounts of a chemical called *tryptophan*, which is closely related to serotonin. So your bedtime glass of milk may be providing a dose of a natural sedative.) If the raphe system of a cat's brain is destroyed, the animal can no longer sleep, no matter how tired it gets.

Another part of the brain stem, the *locus coeruleus*, plays a part in dreaming sleep. Normally you do not move around much during dreams. Your body is limp; indeed, if you are wakened suddenly, you may feel for a moment as though you are paralyzed. Nerve impulses from the locus coeruleus suppress muscle tone and keep the body from acting out its dream fantasies. (If a cat's locus coeruleus is destroyed, it may get up and run around during REM sleep, as though it were catching a mouse or frightened of a dog.)

What makes people wake after they have slept for a certain time? Have you ever found yourself waking up just before the alarm clock rings? Some people can tell themselves the night before to wake up at a certain time, and they wake up at exactly that time in the morning. Scientists believe that the tiny gland in the brain called the *pineal gland* is the timekeeper that helps to control the cycles of sleep and waking. Indeed, the pineal gland produces a hormone called *melatonin*, which acts on the brain cells that use serotonin, the sleep chemical. Melatonin production rises during the dark hours and falls during the day.

What good is sleep? There is evidence that during sleep the body grows and repairs itself. The chemicals that promote such growth and repair are turned off during the day by the action of the hormone *epinephrine*, or *adrenaline*, which acts to stimulate various systems of the body.

Dreaming seems to play an important role in the health of the body. Researchers have tried waking people whenever they begin a phase of REM sleep, thus preventing them from dreaming. Sometimes the volunteers become irritable or have strange drives, such as an uncontrollable hunger. If they are allowed to sleep undisturbed on the following night, they have much more REM sleep than usual, making up the dreams they have missed. Sleep-inducing drugs that change the normal patterns of sleep, suppressing dreaming, can produce a similar "out of sorts" feeling, with an REM rebound when the drug is discontinued. Researchers believe that during dreaming the brain sorts out the various impressions of the day and selects and files away the ones that are important enough to remember. One scientist phrases it in computer terms, saying that dreaming is like "off-line processing": New information is placed in temporary storage in the computer memory until the processing components are available to deal with it. In the "computer" of the brain, that time comes during sleep, when most of the brain's input systems are turned down or off. Then the brain can compare new information with old memories, fit in the bits that are going to be saved, and plan strategies for the future. This processing goes on whether or not we are aware of the dreams, but when we can remember dreams, we can "tune in" to the workings of our unconscious mind.

The study of brain waves has been applied also to some other, even stranger states of mind than sleep. There has been much interest in alpha waves. It has been found that by hooking up a person to an EEG machine with an attachment that can show when the brain is producing alpha waves, the person can learn to produce these waves at will. The machine also may use pickups that record changes in the skin temperature or muscle tension to provide information (feedback) about how relaxed the person is; the technique is called *biofeedback conditioning*. People who have learned to produce alpha waves whenever they want to claim that they feel relaxed and refreshed and better able to do their work during the day.

Classes to teach people techniques of "alpha meditation" have sprung up all over the country. Some use biofeedback machines, whereas others do not. The basic goal of all the techniques is to produce a "relaxation response," and they have proved helpful in the treatment of headaches and various stress-related ailments, such as peptic ulcers. "Alpha meditation" may be similar to the trances into which religious mystics go. (The yogi de-

Biofeedback training: the subject is trying to generate alpha waves.

OTHER STATES OF MIND

scribed in Chapter 4 who was able to control his breathing rate to an astonishing degree showed alpha waves on his EEG as he went into the trance state.)

It is possible to induce a trance state in other people by the technique of *hypnosis.* A hypnotized person may seem to be asleep, but actually the brain waves are those of someone who is alert and awake. Hypnosis permits a person to relax and focus attention very narrowly. This state differs from biofeedback in that the attention is focused outward rather than inward, and the person plays a passive role, obeying the orders of the hypnotist. It is a common but inaccurate belief that only stupid or gullible people can be hypnotized; actually, going into a hypnotic trance requires a fine degree of concentration. Under hypnosis a person may be able to perform feats of strength that would be impossible under normal conditions. The mind can be guided to reduce its awareness of pain to such a degree that surgical operations can be performed without anesthesia. It has been reported that hypnosis can be used to stop bleeding and even to cure some kinds of diseases. Warts, small unruly skin growths, are caused by a virus infection, but they respond very well to hypnosis, disappearing as though by magic under the power of the hypnotist's suggestion.

Probably you have seen demonstrations of hypnosis presented as entertainment on the stage or on television, but the techniques are used also for medical purposes by qualified doctors. Police sometimes use hypnosis to aid in their investigations. The theory is that the greater concentration of a person under hypnosis makes it possible to remember vivid details that cannot be called up in the conscious state. To some degree this is true. In times of stress, such as during a crime, the body is flooded with the hormones epinephrine (adrenaline) and norepinephrine (noradrenaline). There is evidence that norepinephrine, acting as a neurotransmitter in the brain, can work as a "print" instruction, helping to fix memories in vivid detail. But memories formed under great stress may be difficult to recall, because calling them up into the conscious mind also calls up feelings of pain and fear, and the brain defensively suppresses them. Hypnosis helps a person to recall the memories while damping down awareness of the painful emotions that went with them. There is a problem with the recollection of events under hypnosis, however. People in a hypnotic state are extremely suggestible, and the wording of the questions may—deliberately or inadvertently—cause the mind to change remembered details or even invent memories of things that did not happen. For this reason the courts are usually very cautious about accepting testimony obtained under hypnosis, and the use of hypnosis in the investigation of a crime may even discredit the witness's later testimony, given in the conscious state.

Since before the beginning of recorded history, there have been people who claimed to be able to do things that were beyond the powers of the ordinary senses. There have been claims of *telepathy* (reading other people's minds), *clairvoyance* (knowing what is happening somewhere else without any communication by normal means), and *psychokinesis* (causing physical objects to move by mental powers; for example, influencing dice to fall in certain ways or bending a metal rod). People have claimed to be able to find water by *dowsing* with a forked stick, and others have claimed to diagnose or heal ailments by mental powers or to communicate with spirits of the dead.

Usually investigations have revealed some natural explanation, or even a deliberate hoax, but a small number of cases remain that have not yet been explained satisfactorily. Unexplainable feats of these types fall into the category known as *extrasensory perception (ESP)*.

Most scientists have mixed feelings about ESP. They

A standard ESP test for clairvoyance and telepathy uses a special deck of cards.

may concede that there may be something there, but many have the feeling that the subject is not quite respectable. Some serious investigations have been made. A favorite technique is to have the volunteer guess the pictures on cards either held or looked at by another volunteer or by the investigator. A special deck of cards is commonly used, consisting of five each of five picture cards: a cross, a circle, a star, wavy lines, and a square. The cards are shuffled so that they come up in random order. Merely guessing would give an average score of five correct of the twenty-five total answers. Scores much higher than five would be an indication of some kind of ESP operating, and some of the experiments have yielded statistically significant results, even when the volunteer and the investigator are separated by a distance of miles. But ESP ability, if it does exist, is a touchy thing. It does not always work; the results are not regularly repeatable, not even with the same person under the same conditions. This is what makes scientists so uncomfortable about ESP. Normally, they depend on being able to repeat the work of other scientists and get the same results.

It is difficult to speculate how ESP phenomena could work; if they do exist, there are obviously some laws of nature that science has not yet discovered. If the secrets of ESP are ever discovered, it seems fairly certain that they will be found to lie in the human brain.

10
DRUGS
AND THE
MIND

When the IQs of the population are plotted on a graph, the curve looks like a bell. At one end are the few people with very low intelligence, so low that they may never be able to speak or dress themselves. At the other end of the curve are the few people who can learn almost anything with ease. Most of us fall somewhere in the middle part of the "bell." A real mental stimulant could shift the whole curve to the right and make the thin "genius" end much fatter. Researchers are testing various drugs that may improve memory and learning ability, but one genuine mental stimulant is already in wide use. It is not an exotic drug; you may be "addicted" to it yourself.

This mental stimulant is *caffeine*. You probably know that it is found in coffee (unless the coffee beans have been specially treated to remove caffeine). It is also found in tea, in cola drinks (kola nuts contain twice as much caffeine as coffee beans), and in chocolate.

WORLD OF THE BRAIN

Caffeine has two effects on the brain. It constricts blood vessels, reducing the brain's blood supply; so you might expect that the hungry brain would turn sluggish and dull under the influence of caffeine. Apparently this effect is minor in comparison with another type of action: Caffeine stimulates the central nervous system, making transmission of nerve impulses across the synapses more efficient. It gives people a feeling of well-being and makes them feel wide-awake. Studies on both humans and animals show that caffeine actually helps the brain to think and learn more effectively. So it is no wonder that many writers take a cup of coffee to help them to get ideas, and office workers take a coffee break to help them to work better. Coffee also helps to relieve headaches, particularly migraines.

However, this "wonder drug" has some negative effects, too. People who drink a lot of coffee, tea, or cola drinks may be so stimulated that they become nervous and irritable or have trouble sleeping. Caffeine speeds up the heart and also can contribute to the buildup of fat deposits in the artery walls; so caffeine drinks are very bad for people with heart disease. Experiments with animals have shown that caffeine interferes with the repair of damage to *DNA* (deoxyribonucleic acid), the chemical "blueprints" in each cell that direct its activities. As a result, it could possibly contribute to aging, the development of cancer, and the formation of birth defects in fetuses, as all these processes may involve damage to DNA. (This effect has been demonstrated only in laboratory studies, and there is not yet any evidence that it can occur in humans.)

People also can become dependent on caffeine or even addicted to it. Do you know people who never feel "alive" until they have had their morning cup of coffee or tea? Do you ever get a craving for a chocolate bar? A heavy coffee or cola drinker who tries to give it up may actually suffer from withdrawal symptoms. The most common of these is headache. There is a great temptation to reach for a cup of coffee to get rid of the headache, but if the person stays away from caffeine the headaches will go away after a day or two.

Another common drug that affects the brain is *alcohol*. Its effects are opposite to those of caffeine: It is a central nervous system depressant. It seems odd to speak of alcohol as a depressant, when people commonly drink alcoholic beverages to get "high." But the pleasant high that may result from drinking small or moderate amounts of alcohol is actually due to a depression of some of the higher regions of the brain, the rational parts that place inhibitions on the more emotional limbic system. Drunks tend to be very emotional and may change rapidly from cheery high spirits to heartbroken weeping or blind rage.

The depressive effects of alcohol produce a variety of physical impairments. After several drinks, coordination of movements becomes difficult: the hands may shake, and the person may be unable to walk a straight line. A person who drives after drinking is at high risk for an accident, particularly as he or she may not realize that reaction times are slowed and thought processes are confused. After drinking, people also may have trouble controlling what they say, because alcohol has depressed normal inhibitions; and speech is typically slurred and indistinct. Large amounts of alcohol can result in a heavy sleep, from which the drinker awakes with a sick, headachy hangover.

Some people become addicted to alcohol. Unlike the majority of social drinkers, they cannot stop at one or two drinks; once they have started drinking, there is a craving to continue. Alcoholics sometimes experience "blackouts" after drinking, periods during which they cannot remember what they did or said while they were drinking. Alcoholics who try to give up drinking may suffer from a variety of withdrawal symptoms. They may feel deep anxiety, and their bodies shake uncontrollably. While "drying out," alcoholics may suffer from hallucinations (seeing things that are not there). Alcoholics' irrational behavior under the influence of drinking and their constant craving for a drink may make them irritable and undependable, and they may lose jobs, friends, and families, as well as their health.

It is not yet known what causes some people to become alcoholics, whereas others can enjoy occasional drinks in moderation with no ill effects. Studies indicate that actual changes in the brain may be involved in alcohol addiction. In a series of experiments, tiny amounts of alcohol were injected directly into the brains of rats. After a few days, these rats began to choose alcohol instead of drinking water, something that rats normally do not do. These "alcoholic" rats were found to have high levels of the neurotransmitter serotonin. Then the alcohol-addicted rats were given a drug that reduces the serotonin levels in the brain. Immediately they began to drink less alcohol, and a month after receiving the drug they were drinking hardly any alcohol at all.

Alcohol can have even greater effects on the brain when it is combined with other drugs. With *antihistamines* (drugs used for colds and allergies), alcohol can make a person sleepy. With some types of sleeping pills, which are also depressants, alcohol can depress the central nervous system so much that breathing stops and the person dies! Tests of volunteers have shown that a person who drinks and smokes will have a greatly reduced ability to concentrate. This combined effect is much greater than that of either alcohol or smoking alone.

Perhaps you do not think of cigarettes as drugs, but they contain the chemical *nicotine*, which has a powerful effect on the central nervous system. Nicotine is picked up by some of the same nerve cell receptors that combine with an important neurotransmitter, acetylcholine. Nicotine is classified as a stimulant, but smoking can have a relaxing effect. However, nicotine has some negative side effects: It speeds up the heart and constricts blood vessels; smoking has been implicated as a cause of cancer and other lung diseases; and it is addictive.

The caffeine in coffee, tea, and cola drinks; the alcohol in liquor, wine, and beer; and the nicotine in cigarettes are all legal drugs. People take them for their pleasant temporary effects on the brain, and perhaps they do not worry enough about their long-term effects.

There are other drugs that cause effects on the brain that seem desirable to some people. Many of these drugs are either illegal or legal only when prescribed by a doctor in carefully limited amounts for specific diseases. They may provide a pleasant feeling of well-being, an exotic and exciting journey into the "inner mind," or a welcome relief from worries; but they can be extremely dangerous and highly addictive. And, as they are illegal, addicts may be driven to crime to pay for a steady supply of the drugs they need.

The "hard drugs" that are most troublesome in the world today fall into several main groups. Some are depressants. These include the *barbiturates*, which are commonly prescribed as sleeping pills although sleep research indicates that sleeping pills may not provide a "good night's sleep" after all. They tend to suppress the important REM, or dreaming stages, of sleep.

Another class of depressants is the *morphine* family, which includes *opium* and *heroin.* It seems ironic that when heroin was first synthesized, it was thought to be a safe, nonaddictive painkiller that could be used as a substitute for opium and morphine. It was soon found that heroin is extremely addictive and dangerous (an overdose can kill). When a person injects or sniffs a dose of heroin, he or she at first has a feeling of great well-being, a "high" that eventually gives way to sleepiness. Once addicted to the drug, the heroin user cannot go without a dose for very long without suffering uncomfortable physical symptoms and mental anxiety. Soon the user's whole life centers around the need to get and pay for the next "fix." Schoolwork, job, social life, and even eating become unimportant in comparison with the craving for heroin.

Various methods have been tried to help heroin addicts break the habit. Counseling to help them solve the problems that made them turn to drugs seems important. In some areas heroin addicts are given a steady supply of another drug, *methadone.* This drug is a depressant like heroin, and its effects are similar but milder. It has been found that a dose of methadone too small to produce a "high" by itself can block the effects of heroin and help to control the addict's craving for it. Other, nonaddictive drugs also are being used to help addicts break the habit. In Great Britain a different approach to the control of drug addiction is used: heroin is not illegal, but supplies of it are carefully regulated. Addicts who register are given regular free doses of heroin and can live a relatively normal life even with their addiction.

Studies of morphine and other *opiates* (morphinelike drugs) led to a major breakthrough in our knowledge of brain chemistry. In 1973 several research teams, working independently, isolated brain receptors that react selectively with morphine. Scientists wondered why the brains of humans and animals should contain receptors that seemed to be tailor-made for a foreign substance, a chemical that occurs in a poppy plant that grows naturally only in a small region of the world. They theorized that there must be some sort of opiatelike substance produced in the brain itself that would have effects similar to those of the morphine drugs.

Searches for natural opiates soon brought success, and a whole family of them has been discovered. They are a part of the brain's system for coping with pain. Under stress, either physical or emotional, the pituitary gland secretes a hormone called *beta-lipotropin.* In the brain this hormone is subjected to various chemical reactions that split it into fragments. Small fragments called *enkephalins* (their name literally means in the brain) and larger ones called *endorphins* (named for a combination of *endogenous,* or naturally occurring inside, plus morphine), act as natural painkillers. They combine with the opiate receptors and block the pain signals going to the thalamus and higher brain, dulling our perception of pain. They also produce feelings of euphoria, a natural "high." Opiate receptors are found in the largest numbers in the thalamus, in a pain center in the brain stem, and in the amygdala, whose role in emotional arousal explains the "high" that opiates produce.

The discovery of enkephalins and endorphins helped to explain a number of puzzling observations about pain and the drugs used to treat it. For example, when heroin or morphine is taken, it passes into the brain and binds to some of the natural opiate receptors. Because these receptors are occupied, signals are sent to the pituitary, informing it that the natural enkephalins are not needed, and enkephalin production shuts down. As the drug is gradually broken down and eliminated from the body, the receptors are freed, but the pituitary is no longer making enough enkephalin to fill them. If large numbers of receptors are involved, pain messages come through to the conscious part of the brain, and the person feels uncomfortable. Addiction develops as more and more of the *narcotic* (morphinelike drug) is needed to fill the receptors, and between doses the drug user feels an uncomfortable craving for another "fix." If no more of the drug is taken, the discomfort grows into painful withdrawal symptoms that last until the body starts producing enough natural enkephalin again.

Enkephalins and endorphins also are involved in a curious body reaction called the *placebo effect*. Doctors have found that if people in pain are given a simple sugar pill and told that it is an effective painkiller, about a third of them feel much better. Their pain disappears just as dramatically as though they had taken aspirin or one of the other drugs that really do block the pain impulses. The placebo effect works because when people think they have received an effective painkiller, their own bodies produce natural opiates. A drug called *naloxone* also can bind to the opiate receptors but does not work to block the pain impulses. Instead, it prevents natural opiates or narcotic drugs from binding to the receptors and thus blocks their painkilling effect. When people who have been treated successfully with a placebo are given naloxone, their pain comes right back.

Depressants, such as barbiturates and opiates, are a main group of mind-altering drugs that are commonly abused. Another important group is the stimulants. Caffeine is a legal stimulant; cocaine and amphetamines are the stimulants most often involved in illegal drug use.

Cocaine is a substance extracted from dried cocoa leaves. Unlike heroin, which is usually injected, drug abusers typically "snort" cocaine, sniffing it up into the nostrils. It is absorbed through the delicate lining of the nose and produces a "rush" of euphoria. The user becomes excited and talkative; but large doses and continued use can lead to deep depression.

Studies have shown that cocaine works by causing neurons in the brain to release neurotransmitters—serotonin, norepinephrine, and dopamine, which flood the brain cells and produce a flow of nerve impulses that are felt as a euphoric high. Normally, neurotransmitters are reabsorbed promptly by the sending cells as soon as they have transmitted their messages. Cocaine interferes with this natural uptake process, leaving extra amounts of neurotransmitters floating around in the synapses. The receiving cells respond by forming more receptors. If a person takes cocaine frequently, the sending cells cannot produce enough neurotransmitters to satisfy all the receptors, and a craving for more of the drug results.

It was once thought that cocaine was not a very dangerous drug and that it was not addictive. Its use became fashionable in many levels of society, including some wealthy and famous people. Now it is known that co-caine is actually more dangerous and more addictive than heroin. If animals are allowed to take as much of a drug as they wish, about 10 to 15 percent of them become ad-dicted to heroin—roughly the same percentage as human drinkers who become alcoholics. But among animals given free access to cocaine, *all* of them become addicted. Gradually they take more and more of the drug until they are ignoring food, water, sex, and everything else; even-tually they die. In human users repeated use of cocaine can cause severe mental illness, and overdoses can kill.

Recently medical researchers have reported promising results in the treatment of cocaine addicts with a combi-nation of antidepressant drugs and amino-acid building blocks of the neurotransmitters. Gradually the addicts lose their craving for the drug, and some report that co-caine no longer produces euphoria. It is believed that the antidepressant works by crowding out cocaine from the receptors in the brain cells and by promoting a gradual decrease in the number of receptors; meanwhile, the amino acids provide raw materials for the production of neurotransmitters and help to reduce the craving.

Amphetamines are one of the most widely abused types of stimulants. This family of drugs includes ampheta-mine itself (Benzedrine, or "bennies") and related com-pounds such as methamphetamine ("speed"). Billions of amphetamine pills are produced each year. Some are prescribed legally by doctors for various conditions, such as hyperactivity in children and narcolepsy (a condition in which the person suddenly and uncontrollably falls asleep at various times during the day). Amphetamines were used widely as diet pills until it became clear that these drugs do not always reduce the appetite and have serious side effects. A person who takes amphetamines has an immediate feeling of well-being; he or she feels wide-awake and alert and far more intelligent and creative. Students sometimes take amphetamines to get them through final exams; but tests show that amphetamine users' judgment and abilities often are not as good as they think they are.

Amphetamines work by increasing the release of the neurotransmitter norepinephrine from the brain cells and preventing this chemical from being reabsorbed. The extra supplies of the stimulating neurotransmitter make the amphetamine user's brain extremely active and overexcited. The user may be nervous and unable to sleep and then may plunge into deep despair.

As with other drugs, the body quickly builds up a *tolerance* to amphetamines. That is, each time it is used, a larger amount of the drug is needed to produce the same pleasant "high." With long use, amphetamine abusers tend to become unstable. They may have hallucinations and delusions—perhaps thinking that people are plotting against them—and they may become violent.

Another class of drugs that works on the mind is the *psychedelics*, mood-altering drugs that can change and distort perceptions. *Hallucinogens* are drugs that people take deliberately to distort their thoughts and to see strange

DRUGS AND THE MIND

"visions." Some of them are natural products produced by plants, such as nutmeg, *mescaline* (from a form of cactus called peyote), and *psylocybin* (from a type of mushroom). Others, such as *LSD* (lysergic acid diethylamide) and *angel dust (PCP)*, are synthetic substances, produced by chemical reactions. The hallucinations produced by drugs such as LSD and mescaline may be extremely pleasant, or they may be frightening nightmares. The effects of such drugs seem very similar to actual madness produced by mental illnesses such as schizophrenia, and LSD delusions may lead a person to violent acts. A class of drugs called *phenothiazines* have proved useful both in counteracting the effects of LSD and in the treatment of schizophrenia.

Scientists have found that part of the LSD molecule is chemically very similar to the natural brain neurotransmitter serotonin. They believe that LSD molecules may "fool" some structures that normally react with serotonin and thus interfere with the normal working of the brain cells.

The effects of LSD on the brain may be long-lasting. Users have reported that attacks of hallucinations may recur suddenly, months or even years after they last took the drug.

Everyone agrees that barbiturates, heroin, amphetamines, and LSD can be very dangerous when they are taken "for kicks." But there is a widespread debate about another mind drug, *marijuana*. This drug is extracted from wild hemp, a common weed, and its active ingredient is a chemical called *THC* (tetrahydrocannabinol). Marijuana is commonly eaten or smoked, and it produces a variety of effects. It can act as a stimulant or a relaxant; it may bring a pleasant feeling of well-being or may produce hallucinations. The drug seems to distort sense of time and may also change other brain and body reactions. Like alcohol, it impairs physical coordination and judgment; it also interferes with the ability to do mental tasks that depend on the formation of short-term memory. (Long-term memory is not affected.) Active ingredients of marijuana remain in the brain for some days after it is smoked.

Some people believe that marijuana is a very mild drug, far less dangerous than alcohol, and they see no reason why its use should be illegal. Yet long-term use of marijuana can result in chronic fatigue, a decrease in sexual potency, and lung cancer; for people with a tendency to be mentally unstable, the use of any mind drug, including alcohol and marijuana, may drive them into actual mental illness.

Even stable people can get into the habit of turning to mind drugs when they have problems. They try to forget about problems instead of solving them, and they may eventually drop out of school or work and out of life.

11
BRAIN
DISORDERS

Have you seen the TV commercial for a headache remedy where little demons with hammers pound on a person's head? When you have a headache, it sometimes does feel as though there were little demons pounding on your skull. Headaches can come as blinding pains that seem to knife through your brain or as a dull ache that lingers on, making you feel miserable. They may strike the front of your head, the forehead, just behind the eyes, the top or back of your head. Sometimes there seems to be an imaginary band tightened around the head. Often a headache seems to be concentrated on just one side.

When you have a headache, it is not your brain that is hurting, for the nerve cells of the brain are insensitive to pain. Usually the pain of a headache is caused by tense contractions in the muscles of the scalp, by swollen blood vessels in the head, or by stretching or irritation of the *meninges*, the membranes that cover and protect the brain.

WORLD OF THE BRAIN

Headaches are not really diseases, but rather symptoms of diseases or other disorders. They can be caused by a variety of things. A toothache or an infection somewhere else in the body can cause headaches. A bad cold can block up the sinuses behind the nose and cause a painful sinus headache. Alcohol probably causes headaches by irritating the meninges, for it is a poison that is quickly absorbed into the bloodstream and distributed all over the body. Headaches caused by eyestrain usually can be cured by getting the right pair of glasses. Headaches may also be a danger signal, warning of a tumor growing somewhere in the brain.

Specific physical causes such as those just described actually are responsible for only a small minority of headaches. About eight to ten percent fall into the category of *vascular headaches* (migraines). The pain of a migraine is typically very intense and occurs on one side of the head. (The term migraine comes from words meaning half a head.) Sometimes there are warning signals before the headache strikes, such as spots before the eyes and a feeling of nausea. Migraines often run in families, and doctors now believe that the brains of these people may react in an unusual way to little stresses, like failing a test or food allergies. The reaction causes the blood vessels in the brain to swell and produce a blinding headache. Migraine headaches often strike a person again and again. Their effects may last for a day or two, leaving the headache sufferer sick and weak. For migraine attacks preceded by warning signals, the pain of the headache may be prevented by taking a medicine that causes blood vessels to narrow (such as caffeine or a drug called ergot) immediately at the first warning signs. Once the headache has started, sleep may help to relieve the pain.

The vast majority of headaches are *muscle-contraction,* or *tension headaches.* The average person thinks of "tension" as a synonym for stress, and the various stresses of life are common causes of headaches. But in referring to headaches of this type, doctors also have in mind the tension of contracted muscles in the scalp. Usually the pain of a tension headache is a dull ache rather than the sharp and often throbbing pain of a migraine, and it is felt on both sides of the head, often in the back or forehead or temples. Poor posture habits and arthritis of the neck or jaw can be causes of tension headaches, and they can result also from the involuntary tensing of the head and neck muscles against pain. Migraine sufferers also may have tension headaches following the painful migraine attacks. During a tension headache, muscles of the head and neck are contracted and at the same time are being partially starved of oxygen and food materials, because the blood vessels supplying the muscles are tightly constricted. Alcohol, which widens the blood vessels, can help to ease a tension headache (but makes a migraine worse). Warm compresses also can help to relax the muscles and ease the pain. (Cold compresses are good for migraines.)

Doctors use a variety of pain-relieving drugs to treat severe or chronic headache problems. Another approach that is sometimes helpful is biofeedback training. Migraine patients learn to relieve their headaches by directing the flow of blood out of the swollen blood vessels in the head and down into the hands. Temperature sensors on the skin of the hands inform the person of changes in the blood flow; the hands of the migraine sufferer are typically very cold during an attack but warm up as blood flows down into them. Tension headache sufferers are trained to relax their tense head and neck muscles with the aid of feedback from pickups that respond to changes in muscle tension.

Most headaches are not severe or frequent enough to complain to a doctor; sufferers treat themselves by taking aspirin or one of the aspirin substitutes, such as *acetaminophen* (Tylenol, for example) or *ibuprophen* (Advil or Nuprin). Actually, these are the drugs that doctors most often recommend for headaches, too, and they are usually quite effective. Studies on cancer patients troubled with severe pain have shown that aspirin is a more effective painkiller than other more expensive drugs. Aspirin works by blocking natural pain chemicals called *kinins*, which are released when tissues are irritated. It stops the body from making hormones called *prostaglandins*, which cause fever and headaches. Acetaminophen and ibuprophen also block prostaglandin production. Aspirin also cuts down the activity of the blood platelets, tiny structures that take part in the formation of blood clots and are involved in migraine headaches as well. A study of brain waves showed that aspirin has an effect very similar to that of some tranquilizers.

BRAIN DISORDERS

People who suffer from recurring headaches often worry that they may have a brain tumor. Although brain tumors can cause headaches, they are fortunately rather rare: One headache specialist estimates that a person's chances of developing a tumor that affects the brain are only about one in two thousand. Tumors may be cancerous, growing uncontrollably and spreading into healthy tissues, crowding them out and robbing them of nourishment so that the delicate brain cells die. Some tumors are benign: Their growth is slow and controlled over a period of years, and they do not invade the normal tissues or spread to other parts of the body. But even a benign tumor can cause trouble when it occurs in a confined area like the human skull. It can press on tissues, crowding and squashing them. Brain-wave studies and brain scanners are now permitting surgeons to pinpoint the location of tumors without opening the skull; so they can plan an operation to remove the tumor while causing a minimum of damage to the brain structures, or perhaps inject a radioactive substance right into the tumor to destroy selectively the intruding cells. Surgeons in California are using a computerized robot arm to aid in brain surgery. The operations are safer, faster, and less damaging than those performed by human surgeons alone.

Although brain tumors are fairly rare, brain damage due to head injuries is unfortunately rather common. Each year more than ten million Americans are killed or injured in accidents, and many of the injuries are head injuries. Automobile accidents account for a large fraction of this total. Falls and other household accidents can result in brain damage. (Astronaut John Glenn traveled safely into space and back and then slipped in his bathtub at home, hit his head, and suffered from dizzy spells.) Sports can be dangerous at times; in fact, the American Medical Association has called for a total ban on boxing. It is unlikely that sports fans will agree to that, but occasional deaths of boxers after a knockout punch and cases like former champion Muhammad Ali, who suffered from slurred speech and reduced muscle strength and coordination after his retirement, point out the need for more effective protection for the boxers' vulnerable brains.

A punch thrown by a boxer (which can land with a force greater than a thousand pounds) or the impact of a car crash can snap the head back or twist it violently, causing the brain to be slammed against the skull like the yolk inside an egg. Delicate tissues may be crushed, and blood vessels may be stretched and torn. The damaged tissue swells; it is compressed against the unyielding bone of the skull and is damaged further. If vital centers in the brain stem that control breathing and heart action are damaged, instant death can result. Severe head injuries also can result in a *coma*, in which the eyes are closed, the person does not respond to sounds, and there are no voluntary muscle movements. Many such victims die, but others linger and may eventually regain some or all of their brain functions. Prompt medical treatment to

BRAIN DISORDERS

minimize swelling and brain damage is important. Studies have shown that treatment with barbiturates can help, apparently by lowering the oxygen needs of the brain cells and making them less vulnerable to the reduced blood circulation. *Diuretics* (drugs that cause the body to excrete more water) can help to keep brain swelling down. In experiments on animals, amphetamines (which act on the brain's neurotransmitters) have been found to speed up recovery from brain injury, and these drugs now are being tried on human stroke victims. Meanwhile, other researchers are studying *nerve growth factors*, natural brain chemicals that stimulate damaged neurons to sprout new branches. Even with these chemical aids, physical therapy to keep muscles from wasting away and to restore their functions, along with a variety of mental stimulations, are vital in the treatment of brain-injured patients.

Even when a head injury does not seem to have been serious and tests do not show any apparent neurological damage, there may be more subtle and long-lasting effects. After the injury, people may suffer from difficulties with memory, concentration, and abstract thinking; they may become emotionally unstable, impulsive, and irritable, tiring easily and tending to sit around instead of taking part in hobbies or social activities that they once enjoyed. If the person does not realize that there is a physical cause for these problems, they may lead to loss of self-confidence, depression, and difficulties in relationships with family and friends. Both the patients and their families are relieved when the problem is diagnosed and

WORLD OF THE BRAIN

they begin therapy to regain the lost abilities or learn to compensate for handicaps.

Damage to the brain, whether caused by traumatic injury (a blow to the head), a tumor, or a viral infection, may result in *epilepsy*. There may occasionally be a sort of short-circuit in the firing of the neurons of the brain, and the "electrical storm" that follows can spread from one part of the brain to another. Epilepsy may occur in a severe form, called *grand mal* ("great seizure"), in which the body is wracked by powerful convulsions, and the person may lose consciousness. Or the brain may be able to bring the electrical discharges under control quickly so that the person may merely pause for a moment and then resume the interrupted activities, unaware that anything unusual has happened. This milder form of epilepsy is called *petit mal* ("little seizure"). Epilepsy does not affect a person's intelligence. In fact, many famous people have suffered from this disease, including Alexander the Great, Julius Caesar, and Napoleon Bonaparte. Surgical treatments of epilepsy, either destroying the focus that starts the electrical storms or cutting the corpus callosum to prevent the storm from spreading from one hemisphere to the other, have been mentioned already in earlier chapters. Most epileptics do not need surgery; they can eliminate or greatly reduce the number of seizures by taking drugs such as Dilantin, which make the nerve cells of the brain less excitable.

Studies of the chemistry of the brain are pointing the

way to cures for many brain disorders. For example, it was learned that a chemical called *dopamine* serves as a neurotransmitter in brain neurons. Dopamine, like norepinephrine, acts as a stimulant. Then it was discovered that patients with *Parkinson's disease*, or shaking palsy, have less than the normal amount of dopamine in their bodies. This condition strikes about 1% of people over the age of sixty. Patients are plagued by uncontrollable shaking. They may be unable to walk without falling down, and in severe cases they may be unable to talk or even to eat. They cannot be treated directly with dopamine, for this chemical cannot pass through the *blood-brain barrier*, the system that screens out many chemicals in the blood and protects the delicate brain cells from their possibly harmful effects. But it was soon found that a related chemical, L-*dopa*, can pass through the blood-brain barrier. Once in the brain it is converted to dopamine. L-dopa has some drawbacks: It can produce a number of unwanted side effects; its dose must be adjusted carefully for each individual patient; and it does not stop the progress of the disease. But it does relieve the symptoms, and it is bringing new life to many people who were helpless and confined to wheelchairs.

Meanwhile, medical researchers are pursuing two exciting new approaches to the treatment of Parkinson's disease. One line of research was sparked by an unusual accident: In 1982 medical workers in California suddenly began to see patients with severe Parkinson's symptoms—but these were young people, in their twenties or thirties, and Parkinson's disease is a problem of old age. The puzzle was solved when it was discovered that all the young Parkinson's patients were drug addicts who had used heroin contaminated with a chemical called *MPTP*. In the body MPTP is converted to a substance that zooms in straight for a region of the brain called the *substantia nigra* and selectively destroys its cells. The substantia nigra is one of the main dopamine producers in the brain, and Parkinson's patients show an extensive loss of cells in that region; so researchers are now wondering if the condition in elderly people is due to exposure to poisons.

A drug called Deprenyl is known to block the conversion of MPTP to the damaging substance, and it is already being used to treat patients with severe cases of Parkinson's disease. Now researchers are testing the drug to see if it will stop the progress of the condition in patients in earlier stages. Other research teams are trying to cure the disease by transplanting dopamine-producing cells into the brain. A Parkinson-like condition in rats has been treated successfully with transplants of this kind. The operation works best if tissue from embryos or fetuses is used: The transplanted cells grow and connect to the neurons in the brain and produce dopamine. Doctors do not have to worry about careful tissue matching as they do for transplanted kidneys or hearts, because the brain is "immunologically privileged" and is less likely to attack and reject tissue grafts. A Swedish research team has tried to treat human Parkinson's patients with transplants of dopamine-producing cells from the patients' own adrenal glands. A promising, although temporary, improvement was produced; researchers hope that eventually techniques will be worked out to use transplants of brain tissue to treat not only Parkinson's disease, but other types of brain damage as well.

Dopamine also plays a key role in *Huntington's disease*, a hereditary disease that attacks the nervous system of middle-aged people and results in a progressive loss of mental and physical functions. PET scans have shown that in Huntington's patients it is not the dopamine-producing cells that are lost, but rather the dopamine receptors. Even though enough of the neurotransmitter is being produced, the brain cells do not respond to it.

As we get older there is a gradual loss of brain cells, and they are not replaced. The brain may shrink by as much as 20 to 30% between the ages of twenty-five and seventy. Fortunately, people's brains have a great deal of excess capacity, and it is possible to remain alert and intelligent up to the age of one hundred or more. But for millions of Americans, aging has not been so kind. They are victims of *senility*, a progressive loss of memory and other mental functions. A major cause of mental decline in old age is a blocking of the blood vessels supplying the brain, perhaps by a blood clot or a small blood vessel that has burst, bleeding into the brain. Either of these events can result in a stroke, which causes damage to brain tissue. When a large blood vessel is involved, the stroke can cause dramatic effects, perhaps paralyzing one whole side of the body or depriving the victim of the ability to speak. But small strokes due to the blocking of tiny blood vessels may produce effects so minor that they go unnoticed. A person may suffer a series of small strokes, until gradually their effects build up and mental functions decline.

Even more common than this type of senility is *Alzheimer's disease,* a growing menace that currently afflicts at least 2 million Americans and kills more than 120,000 each year. Victims of Alzheimer's disease suffer a progressive loss of memory, which starts with the short-term memory and ultimately reaches the point where they can no longer recall their home, children, and spouse. They become disoriented and get lost easily. Difficulties in understanding spoken and written words develop, and even simple arithmetic becomes impossible. Their energy decreases, and personality changes may occur. Making decisions becomes progressively more difficult, and the Alzheimer's patient tends to avoid new experiences, growing self-absorbed and insensitive to others. As the disease progresses, more and more abilities are lost; patients become unable to bathe, dress, or feed themselves. Eventually they lose control of body functions, and in the final stages paralysis and breathing difficulties develop. In most cases death results from pneumonia.

Studies of the brains of Alzheimer's patients who have died show two very characteristic types of brain damage: *neurofibrillary tangles* (pairs of fine nerve fibers twisted around each other like bits of yarn, lying inside the cell bodies of neurons) and *neuritic plaques* (bits of decomposing nerve cells surrounding a core of fibrous material lying outside the neuron in its terminal branches). The damage is greatest in an area of the forebrain called the *nucleus basalis*, which is the major producer of the neurotransmitter acetylcholine. PET scans and other studies of living Alzheimer's patients show that they do indeed suffer from a lack of enough acetylcholine. The hardest hit are the neurons in the hippocampus, which plays a key role in the formation of short-term memories. Deposits of the metal aluminum, as much as four times the normal amount, have been found in the brains of Alzheimer's patients. Scientists are not yet sure whether these aluminum deposits are a cause of the disease or merely accumulate as a result of other changes in the brain, but it is suggestive that the disease occurs unusually frequently among people living in areas with a high content of aluminum in the soil. (Metals in the soil are taken up by plants that grow in it and eaten by people living in the area.) Alzheimer's disease seems to run in families (one's chances of getting it are four times as high if a close relative is affected), but there is no clear pattern of inheritance. Some studies suggest that an infectious viruslike agent may be involved, and other evidence points to defects of the immune system. So far there are still more questions than answers, and no effective treatment for Alzheimer's disease has yet been found. Approaches now being studied involve attempts to supply the lacking acetylcholine, to remove aluminum from the brain, and to enhance memory with drugs such as vasopressin.

Studies of the brain chemistry are also offering hope in the fight against mental illness. Most of us have a few peculiar habits or irrational fears. In most people these forms of peculiar behavior or attitudes are just minor maladjustments, called *neurotic traits*, which do not prevent them from living a reasonably normal life. A person who is afraid of crowds, for example, can keep mental stress to a minimum by avoiding places where large numbers of people gather. Someone who has an abnormal need to feel clean, washing and bathing dozens of times a day, may be considered odd but will still be able to hold a job and have a family life.

In some people, though, mental illness is more severe. It may prevent them from dealing effectively with other people or with life's problems and chores. They may break out suddenly in a senseless fit of violence or withdraw into a closed little world of make-believe. The serious forms of mental illnesses are called *psychoses*.

Psychoses may take a number of forms. A person may withdraw into a private little world, in which fantasies and hallucinations seem more real than the events of the world outside; eventually contact with the real world is lost. The person may sink into a state of almost complete inactivity or explode into a sudden outbreak of violent rage. These forms of mental illness are called *schizophrenia*. Scientists now believe that the disordered thoughts and hallucinations of the schizophrenic may involve some disorder in the norepinephrine and dopamine system, which excited the brain with more stimuli than it can cope with.

Schizophrenics may begin to have delusions, thinking that everyone is talking about them behind their backs. A television set might be viewed as a spy device. The schizophrenic may feel he or she is a special person, perhaps really some famous person in disguise—a movie star, statesman, or even Christ himself. This variation of mental illness, marked by irrational suspicions and delusions, is the *paranoid* form of schizophrenia.

People commonly think of schizophrenia as a condition of "split personality" (the term literally means split mind) and visualize someone who switches from one personality to another. Actually, however, that is a different kind of mental illness, called *multiple personality disorder*. This is a rare condition in which a person shifts among two or more distinct personalities who may or may not be aware of each other's existence. The personalities typically have very different characteristics: some are "good," others "bad" (sometimes they commit crimes); some have special talents such as musical or artistic ability that the other personalities do not possess. The personalities may be of different ages and even of opposite sexes. Voice and mannerisms change dramatically for each personality. The person is not "faking" the differences; even brain waves and PET scan patterns differ, depending on which personality is currently in control.

In the type of mental illness known as *manic-depressive psychosis*, the patient's moods swing widely. The cycle moves from great elation, when the whole world seems wonderful, to the deepest despair, when it hardly seems worth living at all. In the manic, or elated, phase, the person's brain is flooded with norepinephrine. The mind races, and the manic talks out a flood of ideas that may have little relationship to one another. He or she may be edgy and may easily fly into a rage. In the depressive phase, there is less norepinephrine and dopamine in the brain than usual. The person may sink into a quiet melancholy or may be suspicious and irritable. The depressed person is tortured by fears and guilts and feelings of worthlessness and may try to commit suicide or kill loved ones to "save" them from a life of misery.

The manic-depressives are actually far outnumbered by people who suffer from periodic bouts of depression without an intervening manic phase. Everyone feels depressed now and then, when things are going wrong, but normal depression does not usually last very long, and there is generally a concrete cause. Depression is a form of mental illness when it lasts for weeks or months at a time, when the person is no longer able to enjoy life's normal pleasures, and there is no apparent reason for the depression.

People's attitudes toward madness, or psychosis, have varied according to time and place. Some societies have treated madmen with respect and honor, believing them to be divinely inspired. Others have treated them worse than animals, locking them away in filthy dungeons, without proper food or clothing or any tenderness or care. Only a century ago, psychotics were kept chained in barred cells and beaten or starved.

Even after mental patients were recognized as sick human beings who deserve proper care and attention, there was little agreement as to how they should best be treated. Followers of the Viennese psychiatrist Sigmund Freud practice the technique of *psychoanalysis.* In long talks with the patient, they try to find out what incidents—perhaps buried deep in childhood—may have caused the present problem. However, psychoanalysis may take years, it is extremely expensive, and this technique alone has not been very effective. It cannot be used for many psychotic patients who are so lost in their own private mental world that they cannot be reached by rational discussions.

What is needed for the successful treatment of patients with severe psychoses is a kind of bridge to bring them back in touch with the real world so that they can learn to cope with their problems. One means that has been tried is *electroshock therapy.* Electrodes are placed on the patient's head, and an electric current is sent through the brain. A wave of nerve discharges sweeps through the brain like that of an epileptic attack. Convulsions spread through the muscles of the body. (Injections of muscle-relaxing drugs help to protect the patient from breaking bones.) A patient with severe depression often comes out of electroshock treatment feeling relaxed and relieved. A series of such treatments may leave him or her able to take up a normal life again.

Doctors are not certain why electroshock therapy is effective in a high percent of cases of depression. They believe that the electrical discharges in the brain may raise the levels of serotonin and norepinephrine. But such treatments often cause some loss of memory (usually temporary), and electroshock therapy is an upsetting and frightening experience for the patient.

A promising approach to the treatment and control of mental illness is the use of drugs to normalize the disordered brain chemistry. An old Indian herbal remedy, *rauwolfia*, yielded the drug *reserpine*, the first of the *tranquilizers*. These drugs not only calm excited patients, but also help them to organize their disordered thoughts so that they can be helped to work through their problems. Reserpine is no longer used because of its many undesirable side effects, but the family of tranquilizers has grown until these drugs are perhaps the most widely prescribed group for mental conditions. The phenothiazines have now replaced reserpine in the treatment of schizophrenia and other psychoses. Other tranquilizers, such as Librium, Valium, and Miltown, are frequently precribed for mild "nervousness" or anxiety, and bottles of them can be found in a growing number of bathroom medicine cabinets.

The popularity of tranquilizers for the treatment of mild neuroses worries many doctors. Although these drugs are not addictive in the sense that heroin is, a person may become dependent on them and feel that he or she cannot get along without them. Also, the feeling that unhappiness can be cured by "popping a pill" can lead to experiments with more dangerous mind drugs.

Although tranquilizers can be abused, they have proved to be one of the most effective weapons for psychiatrists in fighting severe mental illness. Most tranquilizers are chemically similar to norepinephrine and dopamine; they work by blocking some of the action of these natural stimulants.

After the discovery of the first tranquilizers, researchers eagerly followed up studies of other mood-changing drugs, and these, too, are helping in the fight against mental illness. *Lithium* salts, for example, are the "drug of choice" for the treatment of manic-depressive psychosis. Lithium belongs to the same chemical family as sodium and potassium, which are active in the transmission of nerve impulses along the neurons. Lithium is active mainly against the manic phase, but when it is taken regularly, it acts to even out the moods somewhat and prevent the up and down swings of the manic-depressive cycle.

A fast-growing group of mind drugs is the mood elevators, which can be used in the treatment of depression. The *MAO inhibitors,* for example, work to correct a chain of chemical reactions in the brain that has gone awry to produce feelings of severe depression. The neurotransmitters dopamine, norepinephrine, and serotonin are all classed in the chemical family of monoamines. The body has another group of chemicals that breaks down monamines when they are no longer needed: the monoamine oxidases (MAOs). If the MAOs are too active, there is a shortage of natural stimulants in the brain, and the person becomes depressed. MAO inhibitors block the action of the monoamine oxidases and thus increase the supply of natural brain stimulants to relieve depression. However, doses of MAO inhibitors must be carefully controlled, and there is an additional complication. Some foods, such as aged cheeses and pickled herring, contain large amounts of monoamines. The body's MAO system normally handles these food chemicals. But if a person is taking a MAO inhibitor, these food monoamines may build up to poisonous levels.

Because of these and other side effects, MAO inhibitors have been largely replaced by another group of mood elevators, the *tricyclic* compounds, such as Elavil (amitriptyline) and Tofranil (imipramine), along with "new generation" mood elevators with fewer and milder side effects.

The use of drugs based on knowledge of the biochemistry of the brain has brought a revolution in the treatment of mental illness, sharply reducing the numbers of people confined to mental hospitals and permitting them to lead normal, productive lives again.

INDEX

Illustrations are in *italics*.

INDEX

INDEX

INDEX

INDEX

intuition, 104
invertebrates, 26
IQ, 126
IQ, racial differences in, 128
IQ tests, 126–128

Kanzi, 35
kinins, 172
Koko, 33

language, 113
lateralization of brain, 95–107
L-dopa, 177
learning, 117, 118, 120
left brain, 98–108
left-handedness, 94, 95, 96
left hemisphere, *10*
Levy, Jerre, 102, 106, 107
Librium, 186
limbic system, 77, *78*, 79, 132, *133*, 137, 157
lithium, 134, 187
lobster, 23
locus coeruleus, 147
long-term memory, 112, 113, 168
love, 137–138
LSD, 167

MacLean, Paul, 131
magnetic resonance imaging, 42
mammal, brain of, *29*
mania, *49*

manic-depressive psychosis, *49*, 183–184, 187
MAO inhibitors, 187–188
marijuana, 167, 168
medulla oblongata, 28, *29*, 61, 63, *65*
melatonin, 148
Memorial Sloan-Kettering Cancer Institute, 57
memorization, 112
memory, 109–130
memory, chemical storage of, 118–119
memory, electrical storage of, 119–121
memory, iconic, 111, 113, 115
memory, long–term, 112
memory, of facts, 109–114
memory, of skills, 109–110
memory retrieval, 123
memory, short-term, 112
memory trace, 121, *122*
meninges, 9, 169
mental illness, 182–188
mental stimulant, 155
mescaline, 167
methadone, 161
methamphetamine, 165
midbrain, 28, *29*, 30, 60, 61
migraine, 156, 170, 171
milk, 147
Miltown, 186
mnemonics, 112, 113, 123
monamine oxidases (MAOs), 187, 188

INDEX

INDEX

INDEX

INDEX